Copyright © 2024 by Maxwell J. Aromano (Author)

All rights reserved. This book or any portion thereof may not be reproduced or used in any manner whatsoever without the express written permission of the publisher except for the use of brief quotations in a book review.

This book is copyright protected. This is only for personal use. You cannot amend, distributor, sell, use, quote or paraphrase any part or the content within this book without the consent of the author. Please note the information contained within this document is for educational and entertainment purposes only. Every attempt has been made to provide accurate, up to date and reliable complete information. No warranties of any kind are expressed or implied.

Readers acknowledge that the author is not engaging in the rendering of legal, financial, medical or professional advice. The content of this book has been derived from various sources. Please consult a licensed professional before attempting any techniques outlined in this book.

By reading this document, the readers agree that under no circumstances are the author responsible for any losses, direct or indirect, which are incurred as a result of the use of information contained within this document, including but not limited to errors, omissions or inaccuracies.

Thank you very much for reading this book.

Title: Dawn of Distrust
Subtitle: Technological Threads Weaving a Trustless Society

Series: Echoes of the Trustless Dawn: Unveiling Humanity's Journey in a World Without Faith
Author: Maxwell J. Aromano

Table of Contents

Introduction 6
The Emergence of a Trustless Society 6
The Technological Tapestry 10
The Promise and Peril 14

Chapter 1: Unveiling Transparency 17
Explore transparency in the trustless society 17
Characters navigate advantages and disadvantages of transparent systems 21
Illustrate impact on governance, relationships, foreshadow conflicts from visibility 24

Chapter 2: Glitches in the System 28
Uncover technological glitches in trustless framework 28
Characters navigate challenges, uncertainties 32
Examine initial responses from society, governing bodies 35
Plant seeds of doubt as the flawless facade cracks 39

Chapter 3: The Ripple Effect 42
Explore glitches' repercussions on society 42
Introduce conflicts from economic instability, disrupted transactions 46
Characters grapple with unforeseen consequences in personal, professional lives 50
Showcase factions advocating different responses to the crisis 54

Chapter 4: Internal Strife 58
Delve into internal conflicts in trustless society 58
Examine ideologies leading to power struggles, fractures in governing bodies 62
Characters caught in crossfire navigating shifting political landscape 66
Explore impact of distrust on alliances, friendships 69

Chapter 5: Human Connections in the Digital Age 73
Explore evolving dynamics of personal relationships in tech-driven society 73
Characters face challenges in friendships, families, romantic connections 77
Illustrate emotional toll of living where human trust yields to technological assurances 81
Highlight resilience, vulnerabilities of the human spirit 86

Chapter 6: Unmasking Secrets 92
Characters uncover hidden agendas, concealed information 92
Explore role of secrecy in society priding itself on transparency 96
Examine consequences of unveiling truths on individual, societal levels 100
Introduce ethical dilemmas, moral ambiguity as characters grapple with newfound knowledge 104

Chapter 7: Crossroads of Faith and Technology .. 108
Explore intersection of faith with rapidly advancing technology... *108*
Characters question balance between traditional values, allure of trustless systems *112*
Examine societal debates, philosophical discussions on consequences of relying solely on technology *117*
Set stage for pivotal decisions shaping the future of the trustless society *121*

Conclusion 125
Summarize key events, developments in "Foundations of Distrust".. *125*
Reflect on characters' journeys, societal impact of trustless experiment *129*
Pose lingering questions, unresolved issues to set stage for subsequent books *132*

Glossary 136
Potential References..139

Introduction
The Emergence of a Trustless Society

In an age defined by rapid technological advancement, the concept of trust has undergone a profound transformation. Traditional systems of trust, rooted in interpersonal relationships and institutional structures, have given way to a new paradigm: the trustless society. This shift, marked by the emergence of decentralized technologies and transparent systems, has fundamentally altered the way individuals interact, govern, and conduct business.

As society hurtles towards an increasingly digitized future, the foundations of trust are being reshaped by technological innovation. The seeds of this transformation were sown in the aftermath of the 2008 financial crisis, a watershed moment that exposed the fragility of centralized institutions and underscored the need for alternative systems of governance. It was within this fertile ground that the concept of a trustless society began to take root.

At its core, a trustless society is defined by its reliance on decentralized networks and cryptographic protocols to facilitate transactions and interactions. Unlike traditional systems where trust is vested in centralized authorities, such as banks or governments, in a trustless society, transactions are executed based on predetermined algorithms and consensus mechanisms, rendering intermediaries obsolete.

The rise of blockchain technology stands as a hallmark of this paradigm shift. Originally conceived as the underlying technology behind Bitcoin, blockchain has since evolved into a versatile tool with applications spanning finance, supply chain management, and beyond. By utilizing a distributed ledger system, blockchain enables transparent and tamper-proof record-keeping, fostering a level of trust among participants that transcends traditional boundaries.

Moreover, the proliferation of smart contracts—a self-executing code that automatically enforces the terms of a contract—has further solidified the foundation of the trustless society. By embedding contractual agreements within immutable code, smart contracts eliminate the need for intermediaries, streamlining processes and reducing the potential for human error or manipulation.

The implications of this technological upheaval are far-reaching, extending beyond the realm of finance to encompass governance, identity management, and even social interactions. In a trustless society, the power dynamics inherent in traditional hierarchies are upended, as individuals reclaim agency over their data and transactions. This newfound autonomy has profound implications for the nature of governance, challenging the centralized authority of nation-states and fostering experiments in decentralized decision-making.

However, the emergence of a trustless society is not without its challenges and complexities. As with any paradigm shift, the transition towards decentralization is accompanied by uncertainties and teething problems. Questions surrounding scalability, interoperability, and regulatory compliance loom large, threatening to impede the widespread adoption of trustless technologies.

Moreover, the erosion of trust in centralized institutions has sparked debates surrounding the ethical and societal implications of a trustless society. Concerns regarding privacy, security, and the concentration of power in the hands of a select few have prompted calls for greater accountability and transparency in the design and implementation of decentralized systems.

Nevertheless, despite these challenges, the march towards a trustless society continues unabated, driven by a shared vision of a more equitable and resilient future. As we embark on this journey of technological evolution, it is imperative that we remain vigilant, mindful of the potential pitfalls and opportunities that lie ahead. For in the dawn of distrust, lies the promise of a new era of empowerment and possibility.

The Technological Tapestry

In an age defined by rapid technological advancement, the concept of trust has undergone a profound transformation. Traditional systems of trust, rooted in interpersonal relationships and institutional structures, have given way to a new paradigm: the trustless society. This shift, marked by the emergence of decentralized technologies and transparent systems, has fundamentally altered the way individuals interact, govern, and conduct business.

At the heart of the trustless society lies a complex web of technological innovations, each thread contributing to the fabric of decentralized governance and transparent systems. From blockchain to smart contracts, these technologies form the backbone of a new era, redefining the boundaries of trust and autonomy.

Blockchain, perhaps the most emblematic of these innovations, serves as the cornerstone of the trustless society. At its core, blockchain is a decentralized ledger that records transactions across a network of computers. Each transaction is stored in a block, which is cryptographically linked to the preceding block, creating an immutable chain of data. This tamper-proof record-keeping mechanism ensures transparency and trust among participants, eliminating the need for intermediaries and centralized authorities.

Moreover, blockchain enables the creation of digital assets known as cryptocurrencies, which operate independently of traditional financial institutions. Bitcoin, the first and most well-known cryptocurrency, was introduced in 2009 as a peer-to-peer electronic cash system. Since then, a plethora of alternative cryptocurrencies, or altcoins, have emerged, each with its own unique features and use cases.

Beyond currency, blockchain technology has found applications in a wide range of industries, from supply chain management to healthcare. In the realm of supply chain, blockchain enables transparent and traceable transactions, allowing stakeholders to track the journey of goods from manufacturer to consumer. Similarly, in healthcare, blockchain facilitates secure and interoperable access to patient data, enhancing the efficiency and accuracy of medical records.

Complementing blockchain is the advent of smart contracts, self-executing contracts with the terms of the agreement directly written into code. By automating the execution of contractual agreements, smart contracts eliminate the need for intermediaries, reducing costs and minimizing the potential for fraud or dispute. This programmable logic opens up a myriad of possibilities, from decentralized finance to decentralized autonomous organizations (DAOs), where decision-making is governed by code rather than human intervention.

In addition to blockchain and smart contracts, other technological advancements are contributing to the tapestry of the trustless society. Decentralized identity solutions, such as self-sovereign identity (SSI), empower individuals to take control of their personal data, reducing reliance on centralized identity providers. Zero-knowledge proofs, cryptographic techniques that allow one party to prove the validity of a statement without revealing any additional information, enhance privacy and confidentiality in trustless transactions.

However, the technological tapestry of the trustless society is not without its limitations and challenges. Scalability remains a pressing concern, as the burgeoning popularity of blockchain strains network capacity and transaction throughput. Interoperability issues also persist, hindering the seamless integration of different blockchain platforms and protocols. Moreover, regulatory uncertainty looms large, as policymakers grapple with the implications of decentralized technologies on traditional legal frameworks.

Nevertheless, despite these challenges, the technological tapestry of the trustless society continues to evolve and expand, weaving a future defined by transparency, autonomy, and decentralization. As we navigate this brave new world of technological innovation, it is imperative that we remain vigilant, mindful of both the promises and pitfalls that lie ahead. For in the interplay of code and consensus lies the promise of a more equitable and resilient society, built on trustless foundations.

The Promise and Peril

In an age defined by rapid technological advancement, the concept of trust has undergone a profound transformation. Traditional systems of trust, rooted in interpersonal relationships and institutional structures, have given way to a new paradigm: the trustless society. This shift, marked by the emergence of decentralized technologies and transparent systems, has fundamentally altered the way individuals interact, govern, and conduct business.

Within the framework of the trustless society, there exists a delicate balance between promise and peril, innovation and uncertainty. On one hand, the potential of decentralized technologies to foster transparency, autonomy, and efficiency is undeniable. Yet, on the other hand, the rapid pace of technological advancement poses significant challenges and risks that must be carefully navigated.

At the heart of the promise of the trustless society lies the democratization of access and opportunity. By removing barriers to entry and intermediaries, decentralized technologies empower individuals to participate in economic and governance systems on their own terms. Financial services, once reserved for the privileged few, are now accessible to anyone with an internet connection, opening up avenues for financial inclusion and empowerment.

Moreover, the transparency inherent in blockchain and other decentralized technologies serves as a bulwark against corruption and fraud. By providing a tamper-proof record of transactions, blockchain enables accountability and trust among participants, fostering a more equitable and just society. From fairer elections to transparent supply chains, the potential applications of transparent systems are vast and far-reaching.

However, alongside the promise of the trustless society looms the specter of peril, as technological innovation outpaces regulatory oversight and societal readiness. One of the most pressing concerns is the potential for privacy violations and surveillance in a world where transactions are recorded on a public ledger. While blockchain offers pseudonymity, ensuring the privacy of sensitive information remains a formidable challenge, particularly in the face of sophisticated surveillance technologies.

Moreover, the decentralization of power inherent in the trustless society raises questions about governance and accountability. In the absence of centralized authorities, decision-making processes become distributed among a network of participants, making it difficult to pinpoint responsibility in the event of malfeasance or misconduct. This diffusion of accountability can give rise to governance challenges and regulatory gaps that threaten the stability and integrity of decentralized systems.

Furthermore, the nascent nature of decentralized technologies makes them susceptible to exploitation and manipulation by bad actors. From hacking attacks targeting cryptocurrency exchanges to fraudulent initial coin offerings (ICOs), the trustless society is not immune to the same pitfalls and vulnerabilities that plague traditional systems. As such, robust security measures and vigilant oversight are essential to safeguarding the integrity and resilience of decentralized ecosystems.

Despite these challenges, the promise of the trustless society continues to inspire innovation and experimentation, as technologists, entrepreneurs, and policymakers grapple with the complexities of decentralization. By embracing the principles of transparency, autonomy, and accountability, we can harness the transformative potential of decentralized technologies to build a more equitable, inclusive, and resilient society. However, it is imperative that we proceed with caution, mindful of the risks and pitfalls that lie ahead. For in the delicate balance between promise and peril lies the future of the trustless society, waiting to be shaped by the choices we make today.

Chapter 1: Unveiling Transparency
Explore transparency in the trustless society

In the tapestry of the trustless society, transparency emerges as a guiding principle, a beacon illuminating the path towards accountability and trust. Yet, beneath its seemingly pristine facade lies a complex interplay of advantages and challenges, as individuals and institutions navigate the nuances of transparent systems.

Transparency, in the context of the trustless society, transcends mere visibility; it embodies a commitment to openness, integrity, and accountability. At its core, transparency is the cornerstone upon which decentralized systems are built, providing a window into the inner workings of transactions, contracts, and governance mechanisms.

One of the most compelling aspects of transparency in the trustless society is its potential to foster trust among participants. In traditional systems, trust is often predicated on blind faith in centralized authorities or intermediaries. However, in a trustless society, trust is derived from the verifiability and immutability of transparent systems, where every transaction is recorded on a public ledger for all to see.

Moreover, transparency serves as a powerful tool for combating corruption and malfeasance, as it exposes wrongdoing and holds perpetrators accountable. By shining a light on the flow of funds and resources, blockchain and other transparent systems create a culture of accountability, where bad actors are unable to conceal their actions behind a veil of secrecy.

Furthermore, transparency promotes efficiency and innovation by reducing friction and inefficiencies in transactions and processes. In supply chain management, for example, transparent systems enable stakeholders to track the movement of goods in real-time, reducing the risk of counterfeiting and streamlining logistics. Similarly, in financial services, transparency fosters competition and innovation by providing equal access to information and opportunities.

However, despite its myriad benefits, transparency in the trustless society is not without its challenges and complexities. One of the most significant concerns is the tension between transparency and privacy, as the public nature of blockchain transactions raises questions about the confidentiality of sensitive information. While blockchain offers pseudonymity, ensuring the privacy of personal data remains a pressing challenge that must be addressed through robust encryption and privacy-enhancing technologies.

Moreover, the sheer volume of data generated by transparent systems poses challenges in terms of scalability and storage. As blockchain networks grow in size and complexity, the capacity to process and store transactions becomes increasingly strained, leading to delays and congestion. Scalability solutions, such as off-chain scaling and sharding, are being actively developed to address these challenges and ensure the seamless operation of transparent systems.

Furthermore, the transparency inherent in decentralized systems can sometimes lead to unintended consequences, such as the exposure of sensitive information or the amplification of errors. In the realm of smart contracts, for example, the immutable nature of blockchain means that once a contract is deployed, it cannot be modified or revoked, even in the event of a coding error or unforeseen circumstance. As such, developers must exercise caution and diligence in the design and deployment of smart contracts to minimize the risk of unintended consequences.

Despite these challenges, transparency remains a fundamental tenet of the trustless society, guiding individuals and institutions towards a future defined by openness, integrity, and accountability. By embracing the principles of transparency and harnessing the transformative power of decentralized technologies, we can build a more equitable, inclusive, and resilient society, where trust is not a luxury afforded to the few, but a right enjoyed by all.

Characters navigate advantages and disadvantages of transparent systems

In the tapestry of the trustless society, transparency emerges as a guiding principle, a beacon illuminating the path towards accountability and trust. Yet, beneath its seemingly pristine facade lies a complex interplay of advantages and challenges, as individuals and institutions navigate the nuances of transparent systems.

As the curtains of transparency are drawn back, characters within the trustless society find themselves at a crossroads, grappling with the advantages and disadvantages of transparent systems.

Among the advantages lies the promise of accountability and trust. Characters like Sarah, a small business owner, find solace in the transparency afforded by blockchain technology. With every transaction recorded on a public ledger, Sarah can ensure that her supply chain is free from fraud or corruption, allowing her to build trust with customers and suppliers alike. Similarly, David, a government official, sees the potential of transparent systems to combat corruption and malfeasance within the public sector. By embracing blockchain technology, David believes that government agencies can restore public trust and accountability, paving the way for more efficient and effective governance.

However, alongside the advantages of transparency come the challenges and complexities of navigating a world where every action is scrutinized and recorded. Characters like Alex, a freelance consultant, struggle with the loss of privacy in a transparent society. As his transactions are laid bare for all to see, Alex grapples with the implications of sharing sensitive financial information with the world, fearing the potential for identity theft or exploitation. Similarly, Maya, a privacy advocate, raises concerns about the unintended consequences of transparency on marginalized communities. In her view, the public nature of blockchain transactions could exacerbate existing inequalities, exposing vulnerable individuals to discrimination or persecution.

Moreover, characters within the trustless society must confront the realities of navigating transparent systems in an interconnected world. For characters like James, a software developer, the challenges of scalability and interoperability loom large. As blockchain networks grow in size and complexity, James struggles to reconcile the promise of transparent systems with the practical limitations of processing and storing vast amounts of data. Similarly,

Emily, a researcher studying the social impact of decentralized technologies, faces difficulties in accessing and analyzing data within transparent systems. Despite the wealth of information available on the blockchain, Emily grapples with the challenge of distinguishing signal from noise, navigating a sea of transactional data to uncover meaningful insights.

Yet, despite the challenges and complexities, characters within the trustless society are united by a shared vision of a future defined by transparency, accountability, and trust. As they navigate the advantages and disadvantages of transparent systems, they discover that the true power lies not in the absence of opacity, but in the ability to harness transparency as a force for good. By embracing the principles of openness and integrity, characters within the trustless society pave the way for a future where trust is not a commodity to be traded, but a right to be cherished and protected.

Illustrate impact on governance, relationships, foreshadow conflicts from visibility

In the tapestry of the trustless society, transparency emerges as a guiding principle, a beacon illuminating the path towards accountability and trust. Yet, beneath its seemingly pristine facade lies a complex interplay of advantages and challenges, as individuals and institutions navigate the nuances of transparent systems.

As the veil of opacity is lifted, the impact of transparency reverberates across the fabric of governance, relationships, and societal dynamics within the trustless society. Characters find themselves navigating a landscape where every action is scrutinized and recorded, where the boundaries between public and private blur, and where conflicts and tensions simmer beneath the surface.

In the realm of governance, the advent of transparent systems promises to usher in a new era of accountability and integrity. Characters like Elena, a civic activist, champion the use of blockchain technology to foster greater transparency and participation in democratic processes. With every vote recorded on a public ledger, Elena believes that citizens can hold elected officials accountable, ensuring that their voices are heard and their interests represented. However, the transition towards transparent governance is not without its challenges, as characters like Marcus, a government bureaucrat, grapple with the implications of relinquishing control and authority to decentralized systems. As traditional power structures are disrupted, Marcus fears that transparent governance could undermine the stability and efficacy of established institutions, foreshadowing conflicts between proponents of transparency and defenders of the status quo.

Similarly, in the realm of interpersonal relationships, the impact of transparency is felt deeply as characters navigate the complexities of trust and vulnerability. For characters like Emma, a romantic partner, the transparency afforded by blockchain technology offers a sense of security and reassurance in her relationship. With every interaction recorded on a public ledger, Emma believes that she can trust her partner implicitly, confident that their commitment is enshrined in immutable code. However, for characters like Liam, a privacy advocate, the erosion of privacy in transparent relationships raises concerns about autonomy and agency. As personal interactions are laid bare for all to see, Liam grapples with the loss of intimacy and authenticity, foreshadowing conflicts over the boundaries between transparency and privacy in relationships.

Moreover, the impact of transparency extends beyond the realm of governance and relationships to shape broader societal dynamics and power structures within the trustless society. Characters like Sofia, a community organizer, embrace transparent systems as a means of empowering marginalized voices and challenging entrenched hierarchies. With every transaction recorded on a public ledger, Sofia believes that communities can reclaim agency and autonomy, transcending traditional barriers of class, race, and gender. However, for characters like Javier, a corporate executive, the rise of transparent systems threatens to disrupt existing power dynamics and economic structures. As transparency exposes vulnerabilities and inequalities within corporate hierarchies, Javier grapples with the prospect of losing control and influence, foreshadowing conflicts between advocates of transparency and defenders of vested interests.

Yet, amidst the conflicts and tensions that arise from visibility, characters within the trustless society discover the potential for transformation and renewal. By confronting the complexities of transparency head-on, they begin to unravel the threads of mistrust and deception that have long plagued their world, weaving a future defined by openness, integrity, and accountability. For in the unveiling of transparency lies the promise of a more equitable and just society, where trust is not a commodity to be traded, but a foundation upon which relationships and governance are built.

Chapter 2: Glitches in the System
Uncover technological glitches in trustless framework

As the trustless society marches forward, propelled by the promise of transparency and autonomy, cracks begin to emerge in the facade of decentralized systems. In the shadow of technological innovation, characters find themselves grappling with unforeseen glitches and vulnerabilities that threaten to undermine the very foundations of trust and integrity.

Within the intricate framework of the trustless society, technological glitches lurk beneath the surface, waiting to disrupt the seamless operation of decentralized systems. Characters like John, a blockchain developer, find themselves at the forefront of uncovering these glitches, as they navigate the complexities of coding and protocol design.

One of the most common glitches plaguing the trustless framework is the issue of scalability. As blockchain networks grow in size and complexity, the capacity to process and store transactions becomes increasingly strained, leading to delays and congestion. Characters like Sarah, a cryptocurrency trader, experience firsthand the frustrations of slow transaction times and high fees, as the network struggles to keep pace with growing demand. Similarly, businesses relying on blockchain technology for supply chain management, such as David's manufacturing company, face difficulties in scaling their operations to meet the needs of a global market. As transactions bottleneck and backlog, the promise of efficiency and transparency begins to unravel, foreshadowing conflicts over the scalability of decentralized systems.

Moreover, the issue of interoperability poses a significant challenge to the seamless operation of decentralized networks. As blockchain platforms proliferate and diverge in design and functionality, the ability to communicate and exchange data across different protocols becomes increasingly fragmented. Characters like Emily, a researcher studying the social impact of decentralized technologies, struggle to reconcile the disparate nature of blockchain ecosystems, as they grapple with the complexities of data interoperability. Similarly, businesses seeking to integrate blockchain solutions into existing infrastructure, such as Maya's healthcare startup, face hurdles in achieving seamless interoperability with legacy systems. As siloed data and incompatible protocols hinder collaboration and innovation, conflicts arise over the feasibility and scalability of interoperable decentralized networks.

Furthermore, the issue of security looms large in the trustless framework, as characters confront the vulnerabilities and exploits that threaten to compromise the integrity of decentralized systems. From hacking attacks targeting cryptocurrency exchanges to smart contract vulnerabilities leading to theft and exploitation, the trustless society is not immune to the same pitfalls and vulnerabilities that plague traditional systems. Characters like James, a cybersecurity expert, find themselves on the front lines of defending against these threats, as they work tirelessly to identify and patch vulnerabilities in decentralized networks. However, despite their efforts, the specter of security breaches and exploits continues to cast a shadow over the promise of trust and autonomy, foreshadowing conflicts over the resilience and robustness of decentralized systems.

Yet, amidst the glitches and vulnerabilities that emerge in the trustless framework, characters within the trustless society discover resilience and ingenuity. By confronting these challenges head-on, they begin to unravel the threads of mistrust and uncertainty that threaten to unravel their world, weaving a future defined by resilience, innovation, and integrity. For in the face of technological glitches lies the opportunity for growth and evolution, as characters harness the power of adversity to forge a stronger, more resilient trustless society.

Characters navigate challenges, uncertainties

As the trustless society advances, propelled by the allure of transparency and autonomy, characters find themselves confronting a myriad of challenges and uncertainties lurking beneath the surface of decentralized systems. In the face of technological glitches and vulnerabilities, they navigate a landscape fraught with uncertainty, where the promise of trust and integrity hangs in the balance.

Within the complex tapestry of the trustless society, characters encounter a plethora of challenges and uncertainties as they navigate the uncharted territory of decentralized systems.

For characters like Sarah, a small business owner, the challenge of scalability poses a significant hurdle in the adoption of blockchain technology for supply chain management. As her business grows and expands into new markets, Sarah finds herself grappling with the limitations of blockchain networks to process and store transactions at scale. The promise of efficiency and transparency begins to unravel in the face of slow transaction times and high fees, forcing Sarah to reconsider the viability of decentralized solutions for her business.

Similarly, characters like David, a government official, confront the issue of interoperability as they seek to integrate blockchain technology into existing governance frameworks. Despite the potential for greater transparency and accountability, David finds himself stymied by the fragmented nature of blockchain ecosystems, where disparate protocols and standards hinder collaboration and data exchange. The vision of a more efficient and responsive government begins to fade as David navigates the complexities of interoperable decentralized networks.

Moreover, characters like Emily, a researcher studying the social impact of decentralized technologies, grapple with the challenge of security as they seek to uncover the vulnerabilities and exploits that threaten to compromise the integrity of blockchain systems. Despite the promise of trust and autonomy, Emily finds herself confronted with the harsh reality of hacking attacks and smart contract vulnerabilities that expose sensitive data and undermine user confidence. The pursuit of innovation and progress is tempered by the need to address the fundamental flaws and weaknesses inherent in decentralized systems.

As characters navigate these challenges and uncertainties, they are forced to confront the limitations of transparency and autonomy in the trustless society. For characters like Alex, a freelance consultant, the erosion of privacy in transparent systems raises concerns about autonomy and agency. As his personal transactions are laid bare for all to see, Alex grapples with the loss of privacy and autonomy, questioning the balance between transparency and individual rights. Similarly, characters like Maya, a privacy advocate, raise concerns about the unintended consequences of transparency on marginalized communities. In her view, the public nature of blockchain transactions could exacerbate existing inequalities, exposing vulnerable individuals to discrimination or persecution.

Yet, amidst the challenges and uncertainties that confront characters within the trustless society, there lies the potential for resilience and innovation. By confronting these obstacles head-on, they begin to unravel the threads of mistrust and uncertainty that threaten to unravel their world, weaving a future defined by resilience, innovation, and integrity. For in the face of challenges lies the opportunity for growth and evolution, as characters harness the power of adversity to forge a stronger, more resilient trustless society.

Examine initial responses from society, governing bodies

As the trustless society advances, propelled by the allure of transparency and autonomy, characters find themselves confronting a myriad of challenges and uncertainties lurking beneath the surface of decentralized systems. In the face of technological glitches and vulnerabilities, they navigate a landscape fraught with uncertainty, where the promise of trust and integrity hangs in the balance.

The emergence of technological glitches in the trustless framework triggers a cascade of responses from both society at large and governing bodies tasked with overseeing and regulating these decentralized systems. Initial reactions vary widely, reflecting the diverse perspectives and interests at play in the trustless society.

In the wake of scalability issues plaguing blockchain networks, society grapples with the implications of slow transaction times and high fees. Everyday users, like Alice, who rely on blockchain technology for financial transactions, voice frustration and concern over the growing pains of decentralized systems. They express disappointment at the failure of blockchain to deliver on its promise of efficiency and accessibility, questioning the viability of transparent systems in the face of scalability challenges. Businesses, too, feel the pinch as supply chains are disrupted and transactions bottleneck, leading to delays and increased costs. Small businesses, in particular, struggle to adapt to the limitations of blockchain technology, with some opting to revert to traditional methods of record-keeping and transaction processing until scalability issues are addressed.

At the same time, governing bodies are forced to confront the implications of interoperability challenges for the regulation and oversight of decentralized systems. Regulators like Thomas, tasked with ensuring compliance and consumer protection in the financial sector, grapple with the fragmented nature of blockchain ecosystems, where disparate protocols and standards hinder effective regulation. They struggle to keep pace with the rapid evolution of decentralized technologies, scrambling to develop frameworks and guidelines that strike a balance between innovation and stability. Some regulators call for greater collaboration and coordination among industry stakeholders to address interoperability challenges, while others advocate for more stringent oversight and regulation to protect consumers and mitigate risks.

Meanwhile, security breaches and exploits in decentralized systems trigger alarm bells among both society and governing bodies alike. Users, like Sarah, who have fallen victim to hacking attacks targeting cryptocurrency exchanges, demand greater accountability and transparency from platform operators. They call for improved security measures and better safeguards to protect their assets and data from malicious actors. Similarly, governing bodies face mounting pressure to take action against bad actors and ensure the integrity of decentralized networks. Regulators like Jessica, tasked with investigating and prosecuting fraud and misconduct in the cryptocurrency space, work tirelessly to identify and root out illicit activities. They collaborate with law enforcement agencies and industry stakeholders to develop strategies and tools to combat cybercrime and protect the interests of consumers.

As society and governing bodies grapple with the initial responses to technological glitches in the trustless framework, tensions simmer beneath the surface, foreshadowing conflicts and debates over the future of decentralized systems. Some advocate for patience and perseverance, urging stakeholders to work together to overcome the challenges and realize the potential of transparent technologies. Others call for caution and restraint, warning of the dangers of rushing headlong into uncharted territory without fully understanding the risks and implications. Yet, amidst the uncertainty and turmoil, there lies the potential for growth and evolution, as society and governing bodies navigate the complexities of the trustless society together. For in the crucible of adversity lies the opportunity for resilience and innovation, as characters and institutions alike rise to meet the challenges of a rapidly changing world.

Plant seeds of doubt as the flawless facade cracks

As the trustless society advances, propelled by the allure of transparency and autonomy, characters find themselves confronting a myriad of challenges and uncertainties lurking beneath the surface of decentralized systems. In the face of technological glitches and vulnerabilities, they navigate a landscape fraught with uncertainty, where the promise of trust and integrity hangs in the balance.

The emergence of technological glitches in the trustless framework serves as a wake-up call, shattering the illusion of invincibility and planting seeds of doubt in the minds of characters and society at large. As the flawless facade of decentralized systems begins to crack, characters grapple with feelings of disillusionment and uncertainty, questioning the very foundations of trust and autonomy.

For characters like Alex, a freelance consultant, the revelation of scalability issues in blockchain networks triggers a crisis of confidence in the reliability of decentralized systems. As he struggles to process a backlog of transactions and navigate rising fees, Alex begins to question the viability of transparent technologies in achieving the promise of efficiency and accessibility. Doubt creeps into his mind as he wonders whether the trustless society is built on shaky foundations, susceptible to the same pitfalls and vulnerabilities as traditional systems.

Similarly, characters like Sarah, a small business owner, experience a sense of betrayal as interoperability challenges disrupt their operations and erode trust in blockchain technology. As she grapples with the limitations of incompatible protocols and fragmented ecosystems, Sarah begins to question whether the benefits of transparency outweigh the costs of complexity and uncertainty. Doubt gnaws at her resolve as she contemplates the future of her business and the role of decentralized systems in shaping it.

Meanwhile, security breaches and exploits in decentralized networks cast a shadow of doubt over the integrity of transparent technologies. Characters like Emily, a researcher studying the social impact of decentralized technologies, feel a sense of disillusionment as they uncover vulnerabilities and weaknesses in blockchain systems. As they witness the exploitation of smart contracts and the theft of sensitive data, Emily and others begin to question whether the trustless society can truly deliver on its promise of security and autonomy. Doubt clouds their optimism as they confront the harsh reality of technological limitations and human fallibility.

As seeds of doubt take root and the flawless facade of the trustless society begins to crumble, characters and society at large are forced to confront uncomfortable truths and uncertainties. Some cling to the hope of technological innovation and progress, believing that the glitches and challenges are merely temporary setbacks on the path towards a more equitable and transparent future. Others succumb to cynicism and skepticism, doubting whether decentralized systems can ever live up to their lofty ideals in the face of practical limitations and human error.

Yet, amidst the doubt and uncertainty that pervades the trustless society, there lies the potential for introspection and growth. As characters grapple with their doubts and fears, they begin to confront the complexities and contradictions of transparent technologies, laying the groundwork for a more nuanced understanding of trust and autonomy. For in the cracks of the flawless facade lies the opportunity for resilience and renewal, as characters and society alike navigate the uncertain terrain of the trustless society together.

Chapter 3: The Ripple Effect
Explore glitches' repercussions on society

In the aftermath of technological glitches within the trustless society, the repercussions ripple through every facet of societal structure and interpersonal relationships. As characters grapple with the unforeseen consequences of these glitches, they are confronted with challenges that test the very fabric of trust and autonomy upon which their world is built.

The glitches within the trustless framework send shockwaves through society, triggering a cascade of repercussions that reverberate across economic, social, and political spheres. As the flaws in decentralized systems come to light, characters and institutions alike are forced to confront the harsh realities of technological limitations and human fallibility.

One of the most immediate repercussions of glitches in the trustless society is economic instability. As blockchain networks struggle to process transactions and maintain stability, financial markets experience volatility and uncertainty. Characters like Mark, a cryptocurrency trader, find themselves navigating choppy waters as prices fluctuate wildly and trading volumes plummet. The promise of decentralized finance begins to unravel in the face of market turbulence, shaking the confidence of investors and stakeholders alike.

Moreover, disruptions in supply chains and logistics amplify the economic impact of glitches on society. Characters like Sarah, a small business owner, feel the ripple effects of interoperability challenges as they struggle to source materials and fulfill orders. The promise of efficiency and transparency in supply chain management gives way to delays and inefficiencies, threatening the viability of businesses and livelihoods. As the ripple effect spreads through the economy, characters and communities grapple with the consequences of technological glitches on their financial well-being.

Beyond economic repercussions, glitches within the trustless society also have profound social implications. As transparency and autonomy falter, trust among individuals and communities erodes, giving rise to tensions and conflicts. Characters like Maya, a privacy advocate, raise concerns about the unintended consequences of transparent systems on marginalized communities. The public nature of blockchain transactions exposes vulnerable individuals to discrimination and exploitation, exacerbating existing inequalities and injustices. As trust in transparent technologies wanes, so too does the social cohesion and solidarity upon which society relies.

Furthermore, glitches within the trustless framework have far-reaching political ramifications, as governing bodies grapple with the challenges of regulating and overseeing decentralized systems. Regulators like Thomas, tasked with maintaining stability and integrity in financial markets, find themselves on the front lines of combating fraud and misconduct. The emergence of security breaches and exploits in decentralized networks raises questions about the efficacy of existing regulatory frameworks and the need for greater oversight and enforcement. As the trustless society confronts its vulnerabilities, so too do policymakers and regulators face the daunting task of restoring confidence and trust in transparent technologies.

As glitches within the trustless framework send shockwaves through society, characters and institutions alike are forced to confront the harsh realities of technological limitations and human fallibility. Economic instability, social tensions, and political upheaval test the resilience of the trustless society, challenging its foundational principles of transparency and autonomy. Yet, amidst the chaos and uncertainty, lies the potential for growth and renewal, as characters and society alike navigate the turbulent waters of the trustless society together.

Introduce conflicts from economic instability, disrupted transactions

In the aftermath of technological glitches within the trustless society, the repercussions ripple through every facet of societal structure and interpersonal relationships. As characters grapple with the unforeseen consequences of these glitches, they are confronted with challenges that test the very fabric of trust and autonomy upon which their world is built.

The glitches within the trustless framework send shockwaves through the economy, disrupting transactions and triggering economic instability that reverberates across industries and communities. As businesses and individuals alike struggle to navigate the fallout, conflicts emerge over how to address the challenges posed by disrupted transactions and market volatility.

At the heart of the conflicts stemming from economic instability lies the struggle to adapt and survive in a rapidly changing landscape. Characters like Sarah, a small business owner, find themselves on the front lines of this battle as they grapple with the implications of disrupted transactions on their livelihoods. For Sarah, whose business relies on blockchain technology for supply chain management, the glitches within decentralized systems pose a direct threat to her ability to fulfill orders and meet customer demands. As transactions bottleneck and logistics grind to a halt, Sarah faces the prospect of financial ruin and bankruptcy, forcing her to make difficult decisions about the future of her business.

Similarly, characters like Mark, a cryptocurrency trader, experience the repercussions of economic instability firsthand as they navigate volatile financial markets. For Mark, whose livelihood depends on his ability to trade cryptocurrencies profitably, the fluctuations in prices and trading volumes triggered by glitches in decentralized networks pose a significant challenge. As he watches his investments dwindle and trading opportunities evaporate, Mark faces mounting pressure to adapt his strategies and mitigate his losses. Yet, amidst the chaos and uncertainty, conflicts arise over how best to navigate the turbulent waters of the trustless economy.

Moreover, disruptions in supply chains and logistics amplify the economic impact of glitches on society, exacerbating tensions and conflicts between stakeholders. Characters like David, a manufacturing company executive, grapple with the implications of disrupted transactions on their operations and bottom line. For David, whose company relies on blockchain technology to track and trace goods throughout the supply chain, the glitches within decentralized systems pose a direct threat to his ability to deliver products to customers on time and in full. As orders are delayed and production schedules thrown into disarray, David faces mounting pressure from customers and suppliers alike, leading to conflicts over responsibility and accountability.

Furthermore, the economic instability triggered by glitches in the trustless framework has broader implications for society as a whole, giving rise to conflicts over resource allocation and distribution. Characters like Maya, a community organizer, witness firsthand the disproportionate impact of disrupted transactions on marginalized communities. For Maya, whose advocacy work centers on social justice and equity, the economic fallout from glitches in decentralized systems highlights the stark inequalities that exist within society. As vulnerable individuals and communities bear the brunt of economic hardship, conflicts arise over how best to address these disparities and ensure fair and equitable access to resources and opportunities.

As conflicts stemming from economic instability and disrupted transactions come to a head, characters and communities alike are forced to confront the harsh realities of navigating the trustless economy. Yet, amidst the chaos and uncertainty, lies the potential for resilience and solidarity, as individuals and institutions come together to support one another and forge a path forward in the face of adversity. For in the crucible of conflict lies the opportunity for growth and renewal, as characters and society alike rise to meet the challenges of a rapidly changing world.

Characters grapple with unforeseen consequences in personal, professional lives

In the aftermath of technological glitches within the trustless society, the repercussions ripple through every facet of societal structure and interpersonal relationships. As characters grapple with the unforeseen consequences of these glitches, they are confronted with challenges that test the very fabric of trust and autonomy upon which their world is built.

The unforeseen consequences of technological glitches within the trustless society extend beyond the economic sphere, infiltrating the personal and professional lives of characters in profound and unexpected ways. As they navigate the fallout of disrupted transactions and economic instability, characters are forced to confront the complexities of trust and autonomy in both their personal and professional relationships.

In their personal lives, characters like Sarah, Alex, and Maya find themselves grappling with the implications of disrupted transactions on their relationships and well-being. For Sarah, the small business owner, the stress and uncertainty of navigating supply chain disruptions take a toll on her mental and emotional health, straining her relationships with loved ones and colleagues. As she juggles the demands of running her business amidst economic instability, Sarah finds herself withdrawing from social interactions and struggling to maintain a sense of balance and perspective.

Similarly, characters like Alex, the freelance consultant, experience the ripple effects of economic instability in their personal lives as they grapple with the financial pressures and uncertainties brought about by disrupted transactions. For Alex, whose livelihood depends on a steady stream of clients and projects, the fluctuations in the market triggered by glitches in decentralized systems lead to sleepless nights and anxiety-filled days. As he struggles to make ends meet and support himself and his loved ones, Alex finds himself questioning his choices and priorities, grappling with feelings of insecurity and inadequacy.

Meanwhile, characters like Maya, the community organizer, witness firsthand the toll that economic instability takes on vulnerable individuals and communities. For Maya, whose advocacy work centers on social justice and equity, the disruptions caused by glitches in the trustless framework serve as a stark reminder of the inequalities that persist within society. As she fights to support those most affected by economic hardship, Maya confronts the limitations of her own resources and the challenges of effecting meaningful change in the face of systemic barriers and entrenched power structures.

In their professional lives, characters like David, Mark, and Emily also feel the impact of technological glitches as they navigate the complexities of their respective industries. For David, the manufacturing company executive, the disruptions caused by disrupted transactions pose a direct threat to his business and reputation. As he struggles to fulfill orders and maintain customer satisfaction amidst supply chain disruptions, David finds himself at odds with colleagues and competitors alike, grappling with the implications of economic instability on his professional trajectory.

Similarly, characters like Mark, the cryptocurrency trader, experience the ripple effects of market volatility as they navigate the uncertainties of the trustless economy. For Mark, whose success depends on his ability to anticipate and capitalize on market trends, the disruptions caused by glitches in decentralized systems pose a significant challenge. As he watches his investments fluctuate wildly and trading opportunities evaporate, Mark finds himself questioning his skills and expertise, grappling with feelings of doubt and insecurity.

Moreover, characters like Emily, the researcher studying the social impact of decentralized technologies, confront the unintended consequences of technological glitches on their professional work and aspirations. For Emily, whose research relies on accurate and reliable data from blockchain networks, the disruptions caused by security breaches and exploits pose a significant obstacle. As she struggles to access and analyze data amidst growing concerns about its integrity and validity, Emily finds herself questioning the feasibility and relevance of her research in the face of mounting challenges and uncertainties.

As characters grapple with the unforeseen consequences of technological glitches in their personal and professional lives, they are forced to confront the complexities of trust and autonomy in a world defined by transparency and uncertainty. Yet, amidst the challenges and uncertainties, lies the potential for growth and resilience, as characters navigate the turbulent waters of the trustless society together, forging bonds of solidarity and support in the face of adversity.

Showcase factions advocating different responses to the crisis

In the aftermath of technological glitches within the trustless society, the repercussions ripple through every facet of societal structure and interpersonal relationships. As characters grapple with the unforeseen consequences of these glitches, they are confronted with challenges that test the very fabric of trust and autonomy upon which their world is built.

As the trustless society faces the fallout from technological glitches, factions emerge advocating different responses to the crisis, reflecting the diverse perspectives and interests at play in the decentralized landscape. These factions represent competing visions for the future of the trustless society, each with its own set of values, priorities, and objectives.

One faction, led by proponents of transparency and decentralization like Elena, advocates for greater collaboration and innovation to address the challenges posed by technological glitches. They argue that the glitches within decentralized systems are merely temporary setbacks on the path towards a more equitable and transparent future. For Elena and others, whose faith in transparent technologies remains unwavering, the key to overcoming the crisis lies in embracing the principles of openness and collaboration, fostering a culture of resilience and innovation in the face of adversity.

Another faction, led by skeptics and critics of transparent technologies like Liam, calls for caution and restraint in the wake of technological glitches. They argue that the flaws and vulnerabilities within decentralized systems undermine the very foundations of trust and autonomy upon which their world is built. For Liam and others, whose trust in transparent technologies has been shaken by the crisis, the priority is to address the root causes of the glitches and ensure that similar incidents do not occur in the future. They advocate for greater scrutiny and accountability in the development and implementation of decentralized systems, calling for rigorous testing and oversight to prevent future crises.

Yet another faction, led by pragmatists and opportunists like Marcus, sees the crisis as an opportunity to consolidate power and influence within the trustless society. They argue that the disruptions caused by technological glitches create openings for those with the resources and foresight to capitalize on them. For Marcus and others, whose priorities lie in maximizing profit and minimizing risk, the focus is on exploiting the vulnerabilities exposed by the crisis to gain a competitive advantage in the decentralized landscape. They advocate for strategic alliances and acquisitions, positioning themselves to emerge stronger and more dominant in the aftermath of the crisis.

As these factions clash over competing visions for the future of the trustless society, tensions rise and conflicts escalate, threatening to tear apart the very fabric of their world. Proponents of transparency and decentralization clash with skeptics and critics, pragmatists and opportunists vie for control and influence, and the lines between friend and foe blur in the chaos and uncertainty of the crisis.

In the midst of the turmoil, characters like Sofia, Javier, and Emma find themselves caught in the crossfire, torn between competing loyalties and conflicting priorities. For Sofia, whose commitment to transparency and social justice is unwavering, the crisis represents an opportunity to challenge entrenched power structures and advocate for the interests of marginalized communities. For Javier, whose allegiance lies with pragmatists and opportunists, the crisis offers a chance to consolidate his influence and secure his position within the trustless society. And for Emma, whose faith in transparent technologies has been shaken by the crisis, the priority is to protect her loved ones and navigate the uncertain terrain of the trustless landscape.

As characters navigate the complexities of factional politics and competing interests, they are forced to confront difficult choices and moral dilemmas that will shape the future of the trustless society. Will they stand firm in their beliefs and principles, or will they succumb to the pressures and temptations of power and influence? Will they forge alliances and collaborate with others, or will they go it alone in pursuit of their own agendas? And ultimately, will they emerge from the crisis stronger and more resilient, or will they fall victim to the chaos and uncertainty that threatens to consume them?

In the crucible of factional conflict, characters are tested like never before, their actions and decisions echoing through the trustless society, shaping its destiny for years to come. For in the chaos and uncertainty of the crisis lies the potential for growth and renewal, as characters confront their fears and uncertainties, forge bonds of solidarity and support, and chart a course towards a future defined by resilience and innovation.

Chapter 4: Internal Strife
Delve into internal conflicts in trustless society

Within the seemingly utopian facade of the trustless society, conflicts simmer beneath the surface, threatening to fracture the very fabric of trust and autonomy upon which it is built. As characters navigate the complexities of internal strife, they are confronted with ideological differences, power struggles, and moral ambiguities that challenge their most deeply held beliefs and principles.

At the heart of the trustless society lie deep-seated internal conflicts that threaten to tear it apart from within. These conflicts stem from a variety of sources, including ideological differences, power struggles, and moral ambiguities, reflecting the diverse perspectives and interests at play in the decentralized landscape.

One source of internal conflict within the trustless society is the clash between proponents of transparency and decentralization and skeptics and critics of transparent technologies. For characters like Elena, whose faith in transparent technologies remains unwavering, the trustless society represents a beacon of hope and progress, a utopian vision of a world free from corruption and inequality. Yet, for skeptics and critics like Liam, the flaws and vulnerabilities within decentralized systems undermine the very foundations of trust and autonomy upon which their world is built, casting doubt on the viability of transparent technologies in achieving their lofty ideals.

Another source of internal conflict within the trustless society is the struggle for power and influence among competing factions and interest groups. As characters vie for control over decentralized networks and resources, tensions rise and conflicts escalate, threatening to destabilize the delicate balance of power within the trustless landscape. For pragmatists and opportunists like Marcus, whose priorities lie in maximizing profit and minimizing risk, the focus is on consolidating power and influence to gain a competitive advantage in the decentralized economy. Yet, for idealists and activists like Sofia, whose commitment to transparency and social justice is unwavering, the priority is to challenge entrenched power structures and advocate for the interests of marginalized communities, even if it means risking their own safety and security.

Moreover, internal conflicts within the trustless society are exacerbated by moral ambiguities and ethical dilemmas that arise in the face of technological glitches and vulnerabilities. As characters grapple with the consequences of their actions and decisions, they are forced to confront difficult choices and moral quandaries that test their most deeply held beliefs and principles. For characters like David, the manufacturing company executive, whose business relies on blockchain technology for supply chain management, the temptation to cut corners and compromise integrity in the face of economic pressures is ever-present, leading to conflicts between personal gain and professional integrity.

As internal conflicts within the trustless society come to a head, characters are forced to confront the complexities of trust and autonomy in a world defined by transparency and uncertainty. Will they remain true to their principles and ideals, or will they succumb to the pressures and temptations of power and influence? Will they forge alliances and collaborate with others, or will they go it alone in pursuit of their own agendas? And ultimately, will they emerge from the turmoil stronger and more resilient, or will they fall victim to the chaos and uncertainty that threatens to consume them?

In the crucible of internal strife, characters are tested like never before, their actions and decisions echoing through the trustless society, shaping its destiny for years to come. For in the chaos and uncertainty of internal conflict lies the potential for growth and renewal, as characters confront their fears and uncertainties, forge bonds of solidarity and support, and chart a course towards a future defined by resilience and innovation.

Examine ideologies leading to power struggles, fractures in governing bodies

Within the seemingly utopian facade of the trustless society, conflicts simmer beneath the surface, threatening to fracture the very fabric of trust and autonomy upon which it is built. As characters navigate the complexities of internal strife, they are confronted with ideological differences, power struggles, and moral ambiguities that challenge their most deeply held beliefs and principles.

The trustless society is not immune to the divisive forces of ideology, as competing visions for the future clash, leading to power struggles and fractures within governing bodies. These ideological differences reflect broader debates about the nature of trust, autonomy, and transparency in the decentralized landscape, shaping the direction and trajectory of the trustless society.

One ideological divide within the trustless society centers on the balance between transparency and privacy, as proponents of openness and accountability clash with advocates for privacy and individual autonomy. For characters like Elena, whose faith in transparent technologies remains unwavering, the trustless society represents a triumph of openness and accountability, a utopian vision of a world free from corruption and inequality. Yet, for skeptics and critics like Liam, the erosion of privacy and personal autonomy within decentralized systems undermines the very foundations of trust and autonomy upon which their world is built, casting doubt on the viability of transparent technologies in achieving their lofty ideals.

Another ideological divide within the trustless society revolves around the role of governance and regulation in maintaining stability and integrity in decentralized networks. For pragmatists and opportunists like Marcus, whose priorities lie in maximizing profit and minimizing risk, the focus is on self-regulation and market forces to govern behavior and enforce compliance. Yet, for idealists and activists like Sofia, whose commitment to transparency and social justice is unwavering, the priority is to challenge entrenched power structures and advocate for the interests of marginalized communities, even if it means risking their own safety and security.

Moreover, ideological differences within the trustless society are reflected in the fractured nature of governing bodies tasked with overseeing and regulating decentralized systems. As members of governing bodies grapple with the implications of ideological divides, tensions rise and conflicts escalate, threatening to undermine the stability and integrity of the trustless landscape. For regulators like Thomas, tasked with maintaining stability and integrity in financial markets, the challenges of navigating ideological differences within governing bodies are compounded by the complexities of decentralized technologies, leading to gridlock and paralysis in decision-making.

As power struggles and fractures within governing bodies come to a head, characters are forced to confront the complexities of trust and autonomy in a world defined by transparency and uncertainty. Will they remain true to their principles and ideals, or will they succumb to the pressures and temptations of power and influence? Will they forge alliances and collaborate with others, or will they go it alone in pursuit of their own agendas? And ultimately, will they emerge from the turmoil stronger and more resilient, or will they fall victim to the chaos and uncertainty that threatens to consume them?

In the crucible of ideological conflict, characters are tested like never before, their actions and decisions echoing through the trustless society, shaping its destiny for years to come. For in the chaos and uncertainty of power struggles and fractures within governing bodies lies the potential for growth and renewal, as characters confront their fears and uncertainties, forge bonds of solidarity and support, and chart a course towards a future defined by resilience and innovation.

Characters caught in crossfire navigating shifting political landscape

Within the seemingly utopian facade of the trustless society, conflicts simmer beneath the surface, threatening to fracture the very fabric of trust and autonomy upon which it is built. As characters navigate the complexities of internal strife, they are confronted with ideological differences, power struggles, and moral ambiguities that challenge their most deeply held beliefs and principles.

In the tumultuous landscape of the trustless society, characters find themselves caught in the crossfire of shifting political dynamics, as competing interests and agendas vie for dominance. As governing bodies grapple with the complexities of decentralized technologies and the challenges of maintaining stability and integrity, characters navigate a landscape fraught with uncertainty and danger.

At the heart of the shifting political landscape lies the struggle for power and influence among competing factions and interest groups. As characters like Sofia, Javier, and Emma navigate the complexities of factional politics, they find themselves torn between competing loyalties and conflicting priorities, forced to confront difficult choices and moral dilemmas that will shape the future of the trustless society.

For characters like Sofia, whose commitment to transparency and social justice is unwavering, the shifting political landscape represents an opportunity to challenge entrenched power structures and advocate for the interests of marginalized communities. Yet, as she navigates the complexities of factional politics, Sofia finds herself drawn into a web of intrigue and betrayal, forced to confront the harsh realities of power and influence in the decentralized landscape.

For characters like Javier, whose allegiance lies with pragmatists and opportunists, the shifting political landscape offers a chance to consolidate his influence and secure his position within the trustless society. Yet, as he rises through the ranks of factional politics, Javier finds himself entangled in a web of corruption and deceit, forced to compromise his principles and values in pursuit of power and influence.

And for characters like Emma, whose faith in transparent technologies has been shaken by the crisis, the shifting political landscape represents a test of her resilience and determination. As she grapples with feelings of doubt and uncertainty, Emma finds herself drawn into a world of intrigue and danger, forced to confront her own fears and insecurities as she navigates the turbulent waters of the trustless society.

As characters caught in the crossfire of shifting political dynamics, Sofia, Javier, and Emma must navigate a landscape fraught with danger and uncertainty, where loyalties are tested and alliances forged and broken in the blink of an eye. Will they remain true to their principles and ideals, or will they succumb to the pressures and temptations of power and influence? Will they forge alliances and collaborate with others, or will they go it alone in pursuit of their own agendas? And ultimately, will they emerge from the turmoil stronger and more resilient, or will they fall victim to the chaos and uncertainty that threatens to consume them?

In the crucible of the shifting political landscape, characters are tested like never before, their actions and decisions echoing through the trustless society, shaping its destiny for years to come. For in the chaos and uncertainty of factional politics lies the potential for growth and renewal, as characters confront their fears and uncertainties, forge bonds of solidarity and support, and chart a course towards a future defined by resilience and innovation.

Explore impact of distrust on alliances, friendships

Within the seemingly utopian facade of the trustless society, conflicts simmer beneath the surface, threatening to fracture the very fabric of trust and autonomy upon which it is built. As characters navigate the complexities of internal strife, they are confronted with ideological differences, power struggles, and moral ambiguities that challenge their most deeply held beliefs and principles.

Distrust, like a corrosive force, seeps into the core of relationships, eroding the bonds that once held characters together. In the trustless society, where transparency reigns supreme, suspicions and doubts can fester unchecked, leading to fractures in alliances and friendships that were once thought unbreakable.

The impact of distrust on alliances and friendships is felt keenly by characters like Sarah and Alex, whose once-solid partnerships begin to unravel in the face of uncertainty and suspicion. For Sarah, whose business relies on transparent technologies for supply chain management, the discovery of discrepancies and inconsistencies within decentralized systems triggers feelings of betrayal and disillusionment. As she confronts the harsh realities of economic instability and disrupted transactions, Sarah finds herself questioning the motives and intentions of her business partners, leading to tensions and conflicts that strain their relationship to the breaking point.

Similarly, for Alex, whose livelihood depends on a network of clients and collaborators, the emergence of distrust and suspicion within the trustless society threatens to undermine the foundation of his professional relationships. As he grapples with the implications of technological glitches and vulnerabilities, Alex finds himself caught between competing interests and agendas, forced to navigate a landscape fraught with uncertainty and danger. The once-solid alliances and friendships that sustained him begin to crumble under the weight of suspicion and doubt, leaving him isolated and vulnerable in the face of mounting challenges.

Moreover, the impact of distrust on alliances and friendships is exacerbated by the prevalence of factional politics and power struggles within the trustless society. As characters like Sofia, Javier, and Emma find themselves caught in the crossfire of shifting political dynamics, they must navigate a landscape rife with betrayal and deceit, where loyalties are tested and alliances forged and broken in the blink of an eye. The bonds of trust and camaraderie that once united them begin to fray as suspicions and doubts take hold, leading to fractures in their relationships that may never fully heal.

For Sofia, whose commitment to transparency and social justice is unwavering, the emergence of distrust and suspicion within her inner circle threatens to undermine the solidarity and support she relies on to effect meaningful change. As she confronts the harsh realities of factional politics and power struggles, Sofia finds herself torn between loyalty to her principles and loyalty to her friends, forced to make difficult choices that may have far-reaching consequences for her personal and professional life.

Similarly, for Javier, whose allegiance lies with pragmatists and opportunists, the impact of distrust on alliances and friendships is felt keenly as he navigates a landscape fraught with danger and uncertainty. As suspicions and doubts cast a shadow over his relationships with colleagues and collaborators, Javier finds himself questioning the motives and intentions of those closest to him, leading to tensions and conflicts that threaten to undermine his position within the trustless society.

And for Emma, whose faith in transparent technologies has been shaken by the crisis, the impact of distrust on alliances and friendships is a bitter pill to swallow. As she grapples with feelings of doubt and uncertainty, Emma finds herself questioning the motives and intentions of those she once considered allies, leading to a sense of isolation and alienation that leaves her adrift in a sea of mistrust and suspicion.

As characters confront the impact of distrust on alliances and friendships, they are forced to confront the complexities of trust and autonomy in a world defined by transparency and uncertainty. Will they remain true to their principles and ideals, or will they succumb to the pressures and temptations of mistrust and suspicion? Will they forge new alliances and friendships, or will they retreat into solitude and isolation in the face of mounting challenges? And ultimately, will they emerge from the turmoil stronger and more resilient, or will they fall victim to the corrosive forces of distrust and suspicion that threaten to consume them?

In the crucible of fractured alliances and friendships, characters are tested like never before, their actions and decisions echoing through the trustless society, shaping its destiny for years to come. For in the chaos and uncertainty of mistrust and suspicion lies the potential for growth and renewal, as characters confront their fears and uncertainties, forge new bonds of solidarity and support, and chart a course towards a future defined by resilience and innovation.

Chapter 5: Human Connections in the Digital Age
Explore evolving dynamics of personal relationships in tech-driven society

As the trustless society grapples with technological glitches and internal strife, the dynamics of personal relationships undergo a profound transformation in the digital age. Characters find themselves navigating the complexities of human connection in a world defined by transparency and uncertainty, where the boundaries between the virtual and the real blur and the nature of trust and intimacy is redefined.

In the tech-driven society of the trustless world, the dynamics of personal relationships undergo a profound evolution, shaped by the interplay of technology, transparency, and human emotion. As characters navigate the complexities of human connection in a world defined by digital innovation and social change, they are confronted with new challenges and opportunities that test the very essence of trust and intimacy.

One aspect of the evolving dynamics of personal relationships in the tech-driven society is the impact of digital communication and social media on the nature of human connection. For characters like Sarah and Alex, whose lives are intertwined with the digital realm, the boundaries between the virtual and the real blur as they navigate a landscape defined by constant connectivity and instant communication. As they engage with friends, family, and colleagues through social media platforms and messaging apps, Sarah and Alex grapple with the implications of digital intimacy and the challenges of maintaining authentic connections in a world of curated personas and filtered experiences.

Moreover, the rise of virtual reality and augmented reality technologies further complicates the dynamics of personal relationships in the tech-driven society. For characters like Sofia and Javier, who immerse themselves in virtual worlds and digital environments, the boundaries between physical and digital reality blur as they explore new forms of connection and interaction. As they navigate virtual spaces and interact with avatars and digital entities, Sofia and Javier confront the challenges of forging meaningful relationships in a world where identity and authenticity are increasingly fluid and subjective.

Another aspect of the evolving dynamics of personal relationships in the tech-driven society is the impact of algorithmic matchmaking and digital dating on the nature of romantic connection. For characters like Emma and Mark, whose search for love is mediated by algorithms and data analytics, the quest for a soulmate takes on a new dimension as they navigate the complexities of online dating and digital romance. As they swipe through profiles and engage in virtual courtship rituals, Emma and Mark grapple with the challenges of building trust and intimacy in a world where compatibility is measured in algorithms and chemistry is quantified in data points.

Furthermore, the advent of artificial intelligence and machine learning technologies raises profound questions about the nature of human connection and emotional intimacy in the tech-driven society. For characters like Maya and David, whose interactions with AI assistants and digital companions blur the lines between human and machine, the boundaries of trust and autonomy are tested as they navigate relationships with sentient beings and intelligent entities. As they engage in conversations and interactions with AI avatars and virtual companions, Maya and David confront the complexities of emotional attachment and ethical responsibility in a world where machines can think, feel, and love.

As characters explore the evolving dynamics of personal relationships in the tech-driven society, they are forced to confront the complexities of human connection in a world defined by digital innovation and social change. Will they embrace the opportunities afforded by technology to forge deeper connections and meaningful relationships, or will they retreat into isolation and anonymity in the face of uncertainty and mistrust? Will they navigate the complexities of digital intimacy with courage and resilience, or will they succumb to the pressures of conformity and commodification in the pursuit of love and companionship? And ultimately, will they emerge from the challenges of the tech-driven society stronger and more resilient, or will they be consumed by the uncertainty and ambiguity that defines their world?

In the crucible of the tech-driven society, characters are tested like never before, their actions and decisions echoing through the trustless landscape, shaping its destiny for years to come. For in the chaos and uncertainty of digital innovation and social change lies the potential for growth and renewal, as characters confront the complexities of human connection and forge new paths towards a future defined by trust, intimacy, and authenticity.

Characters face challenges in friendships, families, romantic connections

In the trustless society, where technology permeates every aspect of daily life, the dynamics of personal relationships undergo a profound transformation. As characters navigate the complexities of human connection in the digital age, they face a myriad of challenges that test the bonds of friendship, family, and romantic love.

Friendships, once thought to be steadfast pillars of support, are now subject to the whims of digital communication and virtual interaction. Characters like Sarah and Alex, longtime friends who have weathered countless storms together, find themselves grappling with the challenges of maintaining their connection in an increasingly digital world. As they rely more on social media platforms and messaging apps to stay in touch, they struggle to bridge the gap between the virtual and the real, navigating a landscape where likes and comments replace face-to-face conversations and emojis convey more than words ever could.

For Sarah and Alex, the challenges of friendship in the digital age are compounded by the pressures of daily life and the demands of their respective careers. As they juggle work, family, and personal responsibilities, they find themselves drifting apart, their once-close bond strained by distance and distraction. Despite their best efforts to stay connected, they struggle to find common ground in a world that seems increasingly fragmented and impersonal, where virtual interactions take precedence over meaningful connections.

Similarly, families are not immune to the impact of technology on human relationships, as characters like Sofia and Javier discover firsthand. As parents of young children, they grapple with the challenges of raising a family in the digital age, where screens and devices compete for attention and traditional family values are increasingly challenged by the pressures of modern life. Despite their best efforts to create a nurturing and supportive environment for their children, Sofia and Javier find themselves navigating a landscape fraught with uncertainty and ambiguity, where the boundaries between virtual and real are blurred and the nature of family bonds is redefined.

Moreover, romantic connections are also subject to the pressures of technology and social change, as characters like Emma and Mark soon realize. As they navigate the complexities of online dating and digital romance, they grapple with the challenges of building trust and intimacy in a world where algorithms and data analytics dictate the course of love. Despite their best efforts to find a soulmate in the digital age, Emma and Mark find themselves confronting the harsh realities of modern romance, where compatibility is measured in algorithms and chemistry is quantified in data points.

For Emma and Mark, the challenges of romantic connection in the digital age are compounded by the pressures of societal expectations and personal insecurities. As they navigate the minefield of online dating and virtual courtship, they struggle to maintain authenticity and vulnerability in a world that prizes perfection and performance. Despite their best efforts to find love and companionship, they find themselves confronting the harsh realities of rejection and disappointment, where the promise of digital connection often fails to live up to the reality of human experience.

As characters face challenges in friendships, families, and romantic connections, they are forced to confront the complexities of human connection in the digital age. Will they embrace the opportunities afforded by technology to forge deeper connections and meaningful relationships, or will they retreat into isolation and anonymity in the face of uncertainty and mistrust? Will they navigate the challenges of digital intimacy with courage and resilience, or will they succumb to the pressures of conformity and commodification in the pursuit of love and companionship? And ultimately, will they emerge from the trials of the digital age stronger and more resilient, or will they be consumed by the uncertainty and ambiguity that defines their world?

In the crucible of the digital age, characters are tested like never before, their actions and decisions echoing through the trustless landscape, shaping its destiny for years to come. For in the chaos and uncertainty of technological innovation and social change lies the potential for growth and renewal, as characters confront the complexities of human connection and forge new paths towards a future defined by trust, intimacy, and authenticity.

Illustrate emotional toll of living where human trust yields to technological assurances

In the trustless society, where technology permeates every aspect of daily life, the dynamics of personal relationships undergo a profound transformation. As characters navigate the complexities of human connection in the digital age, they face a myriad of challenges that test the bonds of friendship, family, and romantic love.

Living in a society where human trust yields to technological assurances exacts a heavy emotional toll on characters, as they grapple with the implications of a world where transparency and autonomy are prized above all else. For characters like Sarah and Alex, who have built their friendship on a foundation of trust and mutual respect, the erosion of human connection in favor of technological assurances leaves them feeling adrift and disconnected. As they navigate the complexities of maintaining their bond in an increasingly digital world, they confront feelings of isolation and alienation that threaten to undermine the very fabric of their friendship.

For Sarah, the emotional toll of living in a society where human trust yields to technological assurances is particularly acute, as she struggles to reconcile her faith in transparent technologies with her desire for authentic human connection. As she relies more on social media platforms and messaging apps to stay in touch with Alex and other friends, she finds herself longing for the warmth and intimacy of face-to-face interaction, where words and gestures convey more than emojis ever could. Despite her best efforts to bridge the gap between the virtual and the real, Sarah finds herself feeling increasingly isolated and alone, as the promise of digital connection fails to fulfill the deeper emotional needs that lie at the heart of human relationships.

Similarly, for Alex, the emotional toll of living in a society where human trust yields to technological assurances is palpable, as he grapples with feelings of betrayal and disillusionment in the face of technological glitches and vulnerabilities. As he confronts the harsh realities of economic instability and disrupted transactions, he finds himself questioning the reliability of the systems and institutions that he once relied on to safeguard his interests. Despite his best efforts to adapt to the demands of the trustless society, Alex finds himself struggling to trust in the very technologies that are supposed to ensure his security and autonomy, leading to feelings of anxiety and uncertainty that threaten to overwhelm him.

Moreover, for characters like Sofia and Javier, who are tasked with raising a family in the digital age, the emotional toll of living in a society where human trust yields to technological assurances is felt keenly as they confront the challenges of parenting in an increasingly digitized world. As they navigate the complexities of balancing screen time and family time, they find themselves grappling with feelings of guilt and inadequacy, as the demands of modern life and the pressures of societal expectations weigh heavily on their shoulders. Despite their best efforts to create a nurturing and supportive environment for their children, Sofia and Javier find themselves feeling increasingly disconnected from their family and each other, as the boundaries between virtual and real blur and the nature of parental authority is called into question.

Furthermore, for characters like Emma and Mark, who are searching for love in the digital age, the emotional toll of living in a society where human trust yields to technological assurances is profound, as they confront the challenges of building meaningful connections in an increasingly fragmented and impersonal world. As they navigate the complexities of online dating and digital romance, they find themselves confronting feelings of rejection and disappointment, as the promise of algorithmic matchmaking fails to fulfill their deeper emotional needs. Despite their best efforts to find a soulmate in the digital age, Emma and Mark find themselves feeling increasingly disillusioned and disheartened, as the search for love becomes increasingly commodified and transactional.

As characters grapple with the emotional toll of living in a society where human trust yields to technological assurances, they are forced to confront the complexities of human connection in the digital age. Will they find solace and support in the midst of uncertainty and mistrust, or will they retreat into isolation and anonymity in the face of overwhelming challenges? Will they embrace the opportunities afforded by technology to forge deeper connections and meaningful relationships, or will they succumb to the pressures of conformity and commodification in the pursuit of love and companionship? And ultimately, will they emerge from the trials of the digital age stronger and more resilient, or will they be consumed by the uncertainty and ambiguity that defines their world?

In the crucible of emotional turmoil, characters are tested like never before, their actions and decisions echoing through the trustless landscape, shaping its destiny for years to come. For in the chaos and uncertainty of technological innovation and social change lies the potential for growth and renewal, as characters confront the complexities of human connection and forge new paths towards a future defined by trust, intimacy, and authenticity.

Highlight resilience, vulnerabilities of the human spirit

In the trustless society, where technology permeates every aspect of daily life, the dynamics of personal relationships undergo a profound transformation. As characters navigate the complexities of human connection in the digital age, they face a myriad of challenges that test the bonds of friendship, family, and romantic love.

Amidst the chaos and uncertainty of the trustless society, the resilience and vulnerabilities of the human spirit shine through, as characters confront the challenges of forging meaningful connections in a world defined by transparency and autonomy. Despite the pressures of technological innovation and social change, they find strength in the bonds of friendship, the warmth of family, and the promise of romantic love, as they navigate the complexities of human connection in the digital age.

One aspect of the resilience of the human spirit is the capacity for adaptation and growth in the face of adversity. For characters like Sarah and Alex, who have weathered countless storms together, the challenges of living in the trustless society only serve to strengthen their bond and deepen their connection. As they confront the uncertainties of economic instability and disrupted transactions, they draw strength from their shared history and mutual support, finding solace in the knowledge that they are not alone in their struggles. Despite the pressures of technological glitches and vulnerabilities, they remain steadfast in their commitment to each other, navigating the complexities of human connection with courage and resilience.

Similarly, for characters like Sofia and Javier, who are tasked with raising a family in the digital age, the resilience of the human spirit is evident in their unwavering dedication to their children and each other. Despite the challenges of balancing screen time and family time, they remain steadfast in their commitment to creating a nurturing and supportive environment for their family, drawing strength from their love and devotion to each other. As they navigate the complexities of parenting in an increasingly digitized world, they find comfort in the knowledge that their bond is unbreakable, their resilience unwavering in the face of uncertainty and change.

Moreover, for characters like Emma and Mark, who are searching for love in the digital age, the resilience of the human spirit is evident in their willingness to persevere despite the challenges and disappointments they encounter along the way. Despite the setbacks of online dating and digital romance, they remain hopeful and optimistic, believing in the power of love to transcend the limitations of technology and bring meaning and fulfillment to their lives. As they navigate the complexities of building meaningful connections in an increasingly fragmented and impersonal world, they draw strength from their vulnerability and openness, finding solace in the knowledge that true love knows no bounds, no matter the obstacles in its path.

Another aspect of the resilience of the human spirit is the capacity for empathy and compassion in the face of adversity. For characters like Maya and David, who navigate relationships with sentient beings and intelligent entities, the challenges of forging meaningful connections in a world defined by technology and transparency only serve to deepen their understanding and appreciation of the human experience. Despite the differences that separate them, they find common ground in their shared humanity, drawing strength from their empathy and compassion, their resilience shining through in the face of uncertainty and ambiguity.

Yet, alongside the resilience of the human spirit, characters also grapple with vulnerabilities and insecurities that threaten to undermine their sense of self-worth and belonging. For characters like Emma and Mark, who confront feelings of rejection and disappointment in their search for love, the vulnerabilities of the human spirit are all too apparent, as they struggle to maintain hope and optimism in the face of overwhelming challenges. Despite their best efforts to remain resilient, they find themselves questioning their worth and value, their vulnerabilities laid bare for all to see in a world that prizes perfection and performance above all else.

Similarly, for characters like Sofia and Javier, who navigate the complexities of parenting in the digital age, the vulnerabilities of the human spirit are evident in their fears and anxieties about the future. Despite their best efforts to create a nurturing and supportive environment for their children, they find themselves confronting feelings of inadequacy and doubt, as the demands of modern life and the pressures of societal expectations weigh heavily on their shoulders. Despite their resilience, they find themselves questioning their ability to protect and provide for their family, their vulnerabilities exposed in a world that demands perfection and certainty in all things.

Moreover, for characters like Sarah and Alex, who navigate the complexities of friendship in the digital age, the vulnerabilities of the human spirit are palpable in their fears of rejection and abandonment. Despite their long history and shared experiences, they find themselves questioning the strength of their bond in the face of uncertainty and change, their vulnerabilities laid bare as they confront the harsh realities of technological glitches and vulnerabilities. Despite their resilience, they find themselves questioning their worth and value, their vulnerabilities exposed in a world that prizes transparency and autonomy above all else.

As characters navigate the complexities of human connection in the digital age, they are confronted with the resilience and vulnerabilities of the human spirit, as they grapple with the challenges of forging meaningful connections in a world defined by technology and transparency. Will they find strength in the bonds of friendship, the warmth of family, and the promise of romantic love, or will they succumb to the pressures of technological innovation and social change, their vulnerabilities laid bare for all to see? Will they embrace the opportunities afforded by technology to forge deeper connections and meaningful relationships, or will they retreat into isolation and anonymity in the face of overwhelming challenges? And ultimately, will they emerge from the trials of the digital age stronger and more resilient, or will they be consumed by the uncertainty and ambiguity that defines their world?

In the crucible of human connection, characters are tested like never before, their actions and decisions echoing through the trustless landscape, shaping its destiny for years to come. For in the chaos and uncertainty of technological innovation and social change lies the potential for growth and renewal, as characters confront the complexities of human connection and forge new paths towards a future defined by trust, intimacy, and authenticity.

Chapter 6: Unmasking Secrets
Characters uncover hidden agendas, concealed information

In the trustless society, where transparency is touted as the cornerstone of progress, the discovery of hidden agendas and concealed information sends shockwaves through the fabric of society. As characters peel back the layers of deception and deceit, they uncover a web of lies and half-truths that threatens to unravel the very foundations upon which their world is built.

The discovery of hidden agendas and concealed information is a turning point for characters in the trustless society, as they grapple with the implications of deception and betrayal in a world that prides itself on transparency and autonomy. For characters like Sarah and Alex, whose lives are intertwined with the inner workings of the trustless system, the revelation of hidden agendas and concealed information comes as a shock, shaking their faith in the systems and institutions they once trusted implicitly.

For Sarah, whose business relies on transparent technologies for supply chain management, the discovery of hidden agendas and concealed information within decentralized systems is a devastating blow, shaking her faith in the very technologies that she has championed for so long. As she delves deeper into the intricacies of blockchain technology and smart contracts, she uncovers evidence of corruption and collusion that threatens to undermine the integrity of the trustless system. Despite her best efforts to maintain her composure and professionalism, Sarah finds herself reeling from the revelation, her trust shattered and her faith in humanity shaken to its core.

Similarly, for Alex, whose livelihood depends on a network of clients and collaborators, the discovery of hidden agendas and concealed information within the trustless society is a rude awakening, challenging his belief in the inherent goodness of human nature. As he uncovers evidence of manipulation and coercion within the highest levels of government and industry, he finds himself questioning the motives and intentions of those he once considered allies. Despite his best efforts to remain objective and impartial, Alex finds himself struggling to reconcile the reality of deception and deceit with the ideals of transparency and autonomy that he holds dear.

Moreover, the discovery of hidden agendas and concealed information has far-reaching implications for characters like Sofia and Javier, whose commitment to social justice and equality is unwavering. As they uncover evidence of systemic inequality and injustice within the trustless society, they find themselves grappling with feelings of outrage and indignation, their faith in the promise of progress shaken to its core. Despite their best efforts to effect meaningful change, Sofia and Javier find themselves facing an uphill battle against entrenched interests and vested powers, their trust in the systems and institutions that govern their world eroded by the revelation of hidden agendas and concealed information.

Furthermore, for characters like Emma and Mark, whose search for love is mediated by algorithms and data analytics, the discovery of hidden agendas and concealed information within the world of online dating and digital romance is a sobering reality check, challenging their belief in the possibility of genuine connection in a world defined by superficiality and artifice. As they uncover evidence of manipulation and exploitation within the algorithms that govern their romantic lives, they find themselves questioning the authenticity of their interactions and the sincerity of their partners. Despite their best efforts to find love and companionship, Emma and Mark find themselves confronting the harsh realities of deception and deceit, their trust in the promise of technology shaken to its core.

As characters uncover hidden agendas and concealed information, they are forced to confront the complexities of trust and autonomy in a world defined by transparency and uncertainty. Will they find the strength to confront the deception and betrayal that threatens to undermine their world, or will they succumb to the pressures of disillusionment and despair? Will they embrace the opportunities afforded by technology to forge deeper connections and meaningful relationships, or will they retreat into isolation and anonymity in the face of overwhelming challenges? And ultimately, will they emerge from the turmoil of unmasking secrets stronger and more resilient, or will they be consumed by the uncertainty and ambiguity that defines their world?

In the crucible of uncovering hidden agendas and concealed information, characters are tested like never before, their actions and decisions echoing through the trustless landscape, shaping its destiny for years to come. For in the chaos and uncertainty of revelation lies the potential for growth and renewal, as characters confront the complexities of deception and betrayal and forge new paths towards a future defined by trust, transparency, and integrity.

Explore role of secrecy in society priding itself on transparency

In the trustless society, where transparency is heralded as the bedrock of progress, the revelation of hidden secrets and clandestine agendas sends shockwaves through the fabric of society. As characters delve into the murky depths of deception and intrigue, they confront the paradoxical role of secrecy in a world that prides itself on openness and autonomy.

Secrecy, in a society built on the ideals of transparency and autonomy, is a double-edged sword. On one hand, it serves as a means of protection, safeguarding sensitive information and guarding against exploitation. On the other hand, it can be used as a tool of manipulation and control, perpetuating inequality and injustice under the guise of protection.

For characters like Sarah and Alex, whose lives are intertwined with the inner workings of the trustless system, the revelation of hidden secrets and clandestine agendas exposes the inherent contradictions at the heart of their society. As they uncover evidence of corruption and collusion within decentralized networks, they are forced to confront the reality that secrecy, far from being an anomaly, is an integral part of the system itself. Despite their best efforts to maintain their faith in the ideals of transparency and autonomy, they find themselves grappling with the uncomfortable truth that secrecy, in some form or another, is a necessary evil in a world defined by complexity and uncertainty.

Moreover, for characters like Sofia and Javier, whose commitment to social justice and equality is unwavering, the revelation of hidden secrets and clandestine agendas is a call to action, challenging them to confront the systemic inequalities that perpetuate injustice and oppression. As they uncover evidence of discrimination and exploitation within the trustless society, they are forced to confront the reality that secrecy, far from being a benign force, is often wielded as a weapon of control by those in power. Despite their best efforts to effect meaningful change, they find themselves facing an uphill battle against entrenched interests and vested powers, their faith in the promise of progress shaken by the revelation that secrecy, far from being an anomaly, is an integral part of the system itself.

Furthermore, for characters like Emma and Mark, whose search for love is mediated by algorithms and data analytics, the revelation of hidden secrets and clandestine agendas within the world of online dating and digital romance is a harsh wake-up call, challenging them to confront the reality that trust, far from being a given, must be earned through honesty and integrity. As they uncover evidence of manipulation and exploitation within the algorithms that govern their romantic lives, they are forced to confront the uncomfortable truth that secrecy, far from being a necessary evil, is often used as a tool of control by those seeking to manipulate and exploit others. Despite their best efforts to find love and companionship, they find themselves confronting the harsh reality that trust, once broken, is not easily repaired, and that secrecy, once exposed, can never be fully erased.

As characters explore the role of secrecy in a society priding itself on transparency and autonomy, they are forced to confront the uncomfortable truth that trust, far from being a given, must be earned through honesty and integrity. Will they find the courage to confront the systemic inequalities that perpetuate injustice and oppression, or will they succumb to the pressures of disillusionment and despair? Will they embrace the opportunities afforded by technology to forge deeper connections and meaningful relationships, or will they retreat into isolation and anonymity in the face of overwhelming challenges? And ultimately, will they emerge from the turmoil of unmasking secrets stronger and more resilient, or will they be consumed by the uncertainty and ambiguity that defines their world?

In the crucible of exploring the role of secrecy, characters are tested like never before, their actions and decisions echoing through the trustless landscape, shaping its destiny for years to come. For in the chaos and uncertainty of revelation lies the potential for growth and renewal, as characters confront the complexities of deception and betrayal and forge new paths towards a future defined by trust, transparency, and integrity.

Examine consequences of unveiling truths on individual, societal levels

In the trustless society, where transparency is heralded as the bedrock of progress, the revelation of hidden secrets and clandestine agendas sends shockwaves through the fabric of society. As characters delve into the murky depths of deception and intrigue, they confront the paradoxical role of secrecy in a world that prides itself on openness and autonomy.

The unveiling of truths has profound consequences on both individual lives and the broader societal landscape within the trustless society. As characters grapple with the repercussions of hidden agendas coming to light, they must navigate a complex web of personal and collective consequences, reshaping their understanding of trust, integrity, and progress.

On an individual level, the consequences of unveiling truths are deeply personal and often transformative. For characters like Sarah and Alex, whose lives are intertwined with the inner workings of the trustless system, the revelation of hidden secrets and clandestine agendas forces them to confront their own complicity and culpability in perpetuating deception and exploitation. As they come to terms with the harsh realities of their society, they are forced to reckon with the consequences of their actions, grappling with feelings of guilt and remorse as they confront the truth of their own involvement in perpetuating injustice and inequality.

Moreover, for characters like Sofia and Javier, whose commitment to social justice and equality is unwavering, the revelation of hidden agendas and clandestine agendas is a call to action, challenging them to confront the systemic inequalities that perpetuate injustice and oppression. As they uncover evidence of discrimination and exploitation within the trustless society, they are forced to confront the reality that secrecy, far from being a benign force, is often wielded as a weapon of control by those in power. Despite their best efforts to effect meaningful change, they find themselves facing an uphill battle against entrenched interests and vested powers, their faith in the promise of progress shaken by the revelation that secrecy, far from being an anomaly, is an integral part of the system itself.

Furthermore, for characters like Emma and Mark, whose search for love is mediated by algorithms and data analytics, the revelation of hidden secrets and clandestine agendas within the world of online dating and digital romance is a harsh wake-up call, challenging them to confront the reality that trust, far from being a given, must be earned through honesty and integrity. As they uncover evidence of manipulation and exploitation within the algorithms that govern their romantic lives, they are forced to confront the uncomfortable truth that secrecy, far from being a necessary evil, is often used as a tool of control by those seeking to manipulate and exploit others. Despite their best efforts to find love and companionship, they find themselves confronting the harsh reality that trust, once broken, is not easily repaired, and that secrecy, once exposed, can never be fully erased.

On a societal level, the consequences of unveiling truths are equally profound, reshaping the very fabric of society and challenging the fundamental assumptions upon which it is built. As the trustless society grapples with the fallout from hidden agendas coming to light, it is forced to confront the harsh realities of its own shortcomings and failures, as well as the potential for growth and renewal in the face of adversity.

Moreover, the consequences of unveiling truths extend far beyond the individual lives of characters, reverberating through the broader societal landscape and shaping the course of history for generations to come. As the trustless society grapples with the fallout from hidden agendas coming to light, it is forced to confront the harsh realities of its own shortcomings and failures, as well as the potential for growth and renewal in the face of adversity.

As characters examine the consequences of unveiling truths on individual and societal levels, they are forced to confront the complexities of trust, integrity, and progress in a world defined by transparency and autonomy. Will they find the courage to confront the systemic inequalities that perpetuate injustice and oppression, or will they succumb to the pressures of disillusionment and despair? Will they embrace the opportunities afforded by technology to forge deeper connections and meaningful relationships, or will they retreat into isolation and anonymity in the face of overwhelming challenges? And ultimately, will they emerge from the turmoil of unmasking secrets stronger and more resilient, or will they be consumed by the uncertainty and ambiguity that defines their world?

In the crucible of examining the consequences of unveiling truths, characters are tested like never before, their actions and decisions echoing through the trustless landscape, shaping its destiny for years to come. For in the chaos and uncertainty of revelation lies the potential for growth and renewal, as characters confront the complexities of deception and betrayal and forge new paths towards a future defined by trust, transparency, and integrity.

Introduce ethical dilemmas, moral ambiguity as characters grapple with newfound knowledge

In the trustless society, where transparency is heralded as the bedrock of progress, the revelation of hidden secrets and clandestine agendas sends shockwaves through the fabric of society. As characters delve into the murky depths of deception and intrigue, they confront the paradoxical role of secrecy in a world that prides itself on openness and autonomy.

The unveiling of truths in the trustless society brings with it a host of ethical dilemmas and moral ambiguities, as characters grapple with the implications of their newfound knowledge. As they navigate the complexities of trust, integrity, and progress, they are forced to confront the ethical quandaries that arise when the boundaries between right and wrong become blurred.

For characters like Sarah and Alex, whose lives are intertwined with the inner workings of the trustless system, the revelation of hidden secrets and clandestine agendas forces them to confront the ethical dilemmas inherent in their society. As they uncover evidence of corruption and collusion within decentralized networks, they are faced with the difficult choice of whether to expose the truth at the risk of destabilizing the very foundations of their society or to turn a blind eye in the name of self-preservation. Despite their best efforts to navigate the murky waters of moral ambiguity, they find themselves torn between their desire to uphold their principles and their fear of the consequences of doing so.

Moreover, for characters like Sofia and Javier, whose commitment to social justice and equality is unwavering, the revelation of hidden agendas and clandestine agendas presents a moral imperative to act in the face of injustice and oppression. As they uncover evidence of discrimination and exploitation within the trustless society, they are forced to confront the ethical dilemmas inherent in their pursuit of justice, grappling with the difficult choice of whether to risk their own safety and security in the name of principle or to remain silent in the face of systemic inequality. Despite their best efforts to uphold their values, they find themselves wrestling with the complexities of moral ambiguity, their resolve tested by the harsh realities of their world.

Furthermore, for characters like Emma and Mark, whose search for love is mediated by algorithms and data analytics, the revelation of hidden secrets and clandestine agendas within the world of online dating and digital romance raises difficult questions about the nature of trust and authenticity in a world defined by artifice and manipulation. As they uncover evidence of deception and exploitation within the algorithms that govern their romantic lives, they are forced to confront the ethical dilemmas inherent in their search for love, grappling with the difficult choice of whether to trust in the promise of technology or to reject it in favor of more traditional forms of connection. Despite their best efforts to navigate the complexities of moral ambiguity, they find themselves questioning the very foundations of their relationships, their faith in the possibility of genuine connection shaken by the revelation of hidden agendas and concealed information.

On a societal level, the introduction of ethical dilemmas and moral ambiguity has far-reaching implications for the trustless society as a whole, reshaping the very fabric of its existence and challenging the fundamental assumptions upon which it is built. As the trustless society grapples with the fallout from hidden agendas coming to light, it is forced to confront the ethical quandaries inherent in its pursuit of progress, grappling with the difficult choice of whether to sacrifice its principles in the name of stability or to embrace the uncertainty of change in the pursuit of a more just and equitable future.

As characters grapple with the ethical dilemmas and moral ambiguities inherent in their newfound knowledge, they are forced to confront the complexities of trust, integrity, and progress in a world defined by transparency and autonomy. Will they find the courage to confront the ethical quandaries that arise when the boundaries between right and wrong become blurred, or will they succumb to the pressures of self-interest and self-preservation? Will they embrace the opportunities afforded by technology to forge deeper connections and meaningful relationships, or will they retreat into isolation and anonymity in the face of overwhelming challenges? And ultimately, will they emerge from the turmoil of unmasking secrets stronger and more resilient, or will they be consumed by the uncertainty and ambiguity that defines their world?

In the crucible of confronting ethical dilemmas and moral ambiguities, characters are tested like never before, their actions and decisions echoing through the trustless landscape, shaping its destiny for years to come. For in the chaos and uncertainty of moral ambiguity lies the potential for growth and renewal, as characters confront the complexities of trust, integrity, and progress and forge new paths towards a future defined by justice, equity, and authenticity.

Chapter 7: Crossroads of Faith and Technology
Explore intersection of faith with rapidly advancing technology

In the trustless society, where technological advancements have reshaped every aspect of daily life, the intersection of faith and technology presents a unique set of challenges and opportunities. As characters navigate the complexities of belief and progress, they confront the ever-widening chasm between tradition and innovation, grappling with questions of identity, purpose, and meaning in a world that is constantly evolving.

The intersection of faith with rapidly advancing technology is a terrain fraught with tension and uncertainty, as characters confront the clash between tradition and innovation, belief and skepticism. As they navigate this complex landscape, they are forced to confront the fundamental questions of existence and purpose, grappling with the implications of technological progress on their faith and spirituality.

For characters like Sarah and Alex, whose lives are deeply rooted in the traditions of their faith, the rapid advancements of technology present a challenge to their deeply held beliefs and values. As they witness the rise of artificial intelligence and the proliferation of automated systems, they are forced to confront the question of whether technology can coexist with their religious convictions or whether it represents a threat to their spiritual identity. Despite their best efforts to reconcile the two, they find themselves torn between the comfort of tradition and the allure of progress, their faith tested by the uncertainties of the digital age.

Moreover, for characters like Sofia and Javier, whose commitment to social justice is informed by their religious beliefs, the intersection of faith and technology presents an opportunity to effect meaningful change in their community. As they harness the power of social media and digital activism to advocate for equality and justice, they are forced to confront the question of whether technology can be a force for good in the world or whether it perpetuates the very injustices they seek to eradicate. Despite their best efforts to leverage technology for positive change, they find themselves grappling with the ethical implications of their actions, their faith tested by the complexities of the modern world.

Furthermore, for characters like Emma and Mark, whose search for love is mediated by algorithms and data analytics, the intersection of faith and technology raises questions about the nature of human connection and intimacy in a digital age. As they navigate the complexities of online dating and digital romance, they are forced to confront the question of whether technology can truly facilitate meaningful relationships or whether it erodes the very foundations of love and connection. Despite their best efforts to find love and companionship, they find themselves questioning the authenticity of their interactions, their faith in the possibility of genuine connection shaken by the uncertainties of the digital age.

On a societal level, the intersection of faith with rapidly advancing technology has far-reaching implications for the trustless society as a whole, reshaping the very fabric of its existence and challenging the fundamental assumptions upon which it is built. As the trustless society grapples with the implications of technological progress on faith and spirituality, it is forced to confront the question of whether technology can provide answers to the ultimate questions of existence and purpose or whether it merely raises more questions than it answers. Despite its best efforts to embrace progress and innovation, the trustless society finds itself grappling with the complexities of faith and spirituality, its identity and purpose called into question by the uncertainties of the digital age.

As characters explore the intersection of faith with rapidly advancing technology, they are forced to confront the complexities of belief and progress in a world that is constantly evolving. Will they find the courage to embrace the opportunities afforded by technology to deepen their faith and spirituality, or will they succumb to the pressures of skepticism and doubt? Will they find meaning and purpose in the midst of uncertainty and ambiguity, or will they be consumed by the complexities of the modern world? And ultimately, will they emerge from the crossroads of faith and technology stronger and more resilient, or will they be lost in the ever-widening chasm between tradition and innovation?

In the crucible of exploring the intersection of faith with rapidly advancing technology, characters are tested like never before, their actions and decisions echoing through the trustless landscape, shaping its destiny for years to come. For in the chaos and uncertainty of the digital age lies the potential for growth and renewal, as characters confront the complexities of belief and progress and forge new paths towards a future defined by faith, resilience, and authenticity.

Characters question balance between traditional values, allure of trustless systems

In the trustless society, where technological advancements have reshaped every aspect of daily life, the intersection of faith and technology presents a unique set of challenges and opportunities. As characters navigate the complexities of belief and progress, they confront the ever-widening chasm between tradition and innovation, grappling with questions of identity, purpose, and meaning in a world that is constantly evolving.

The balance between traditional values and the allure of trustless systems is a central theme in the lives of characters within the trustless society. As they navigate the complex interplay between age-old beliefs and cutting-edge technologies, they are forced to confront the fundamental question of whether progress and innovation come at the expense of tradition and heritage.

For characters like Sarah and Alex, whose lives are deeply rooted in the traditions of their faith, the rapid advancements of technology present a challenge to their deeply held values and beliefs. Raised in communities steeped in centuries-old traditions and customs, they find themselves grappling with the allure of trustless systems that promise efficiency and convenience but often at the cost of human connection and spirituality. As they witness the rise of artificial intelligence and the proliferation of automated systems, they are torn between the comfort of tradition and the allure of progress, their faith tested by the uncertainties of the digital age.

Moreover, for characters like Sofia and Javier, whose commitment to social justice is informed by their religious convictions, the balance between traditional values and the allure of trustless systems is a constant source of tension and conflict. Raised in communities where the teachings of compassion and empathy are central to their faith, they find themselves grappling with the implications of technology on their pursuit of justice and equality. As they harness the power of social media and digital activism to advocate for change, they are forced to confront the question of whether progress and innovation can truly facilitate meaningful social change or whether they merely perpetuate the injustices they seek to eradicate. Despite their best efforts to leverage technology for positive change, they find themselves questioning the compatibility of trustless systems with their deeply held values and beliefs.

Furthermore, for characters like Emma and Mark, whose search for love is mediated by algorithms and data analytics, the balance between traditional values and the allure of trustless systems is a central theme in their quest for connection and intimacy. Raised in a society where the pursuit of love is increasingly mediated by technology, they find themselves grappling with the implications of online dating and digital romance on their understanding of relationships and commitment. As they navigate the complexities of algorithmic matchmaking and virtual courtship, they are forced to confront the question of whether trustless systems can truly facilitate meaningful connections or whether they merely perpetuate the superficiality and transience of modern relationships. Despite their best efforts to find love and companionship, they find themselves questioning the authenticity of their interactions, their faith in the possibility of genuine connection tested by the uncertainties of the digital age.

On a societal level, the balance between traditional values and the allure of trustless systems has far-reaching implications for the trustless society as a whole, reshaping the very fabric of its existence and challenging the fundamental assumptions upon which it is built. As the trustless society grapples with the implications of technological progress on its values and beliefs, it is forced to confront the question of whether progress and innovation can truly coexist with tradition and heritage or whether they inevitably lead to their erosion and decay. Despite its best efforts to embrace the opportunities afforded by technology, the trustless society finds itself grappling with the complexities of identity and purpose, its future uncertain in the face of competing visions of progress and tradition.

As characters question the balance between traditional values and the allure of trustless systems, they are forced to confront the complexities of belief and progress in a world that is constantly evolving. Will they find the courage to embrace the opportunities afforded by technology while remaining true to their values and beliefs, or will they succumb to the pressures of progress and innovation at the expense of tradition and heritage? Will they find meaning and purpose in the midst of uncertainty and ambiguity, or will they be consumed by the ever-widening chasm between the past and the future? And ultimately, will they emerge from the crossroads of faith and technology stronger and more resilient, or will they be lost in the complexities of the modern world?

In the crucible of questioning the balance between traditional values and the allure of trustless systems, characters are tested like never before, their actions and decisions echoing through the trustless landscape, shaping its destiny for years to come. For in the chaos and uncertainty of the digital age lies the potential for growth and renewal, as characters confront the complexities of belief and progress and forge new paths towards a future defined by faith, resilience, and authenticity.

Examine societal debates, philosophical discussions on consequences of relying solely on technology

In the trustless society, where technological advancements have reshaped every aspect of daily life, the intersection of faith and technology presents a unique set of challenges and opportunities. As characters navigate the complexities of belief and progress, they confront the ever-widening chasm between tradition and innovation, grappling with questions of identity, purpose, and meaning in a world that is constantly evolving.

The reliance on technology in the trustless society has sparked intense societal debates and philosophical discussions about the consequences of placing undue trust in technological systems. As characters grapple with the implications of a society increasingly governed by algorithms and automated processes, they are forced to confront the ethical, moral, and existential dilemmas that arise when humanity cedes control to machines.

One of the central debates in the trustless society revolves around the question of autonomy and agency in an increasingly technologically mediated world. Critics argue that the widespread adoption of automated systems and artificial intelligence erodes individual freedom and autonomy, relegating humans to the role of passive spectators in their own lives. They raise concerns about the loss of human agency in decision-making processes, as algorithms and machine learning algorithms increasingly dictate the course of action in various domains, from healthcare to finance. This debate prompts characters like Sarah and Alex to question the extent to which they are willing to relinquish control to technological systems, grappling with the ethical implications of placing blind trust in algorithms and automated processes.

Moreover, societal debates in the trustless society also center around the ethical dimensions of technology, particularly in relation to issues of privacy, surveillance, and data ownership. As technological advancements enable the collection and analysis of vast amounts of personal data, questions arise about the ethical use of this information and the potential for abuse by corporations and governments. Characters like Sofia and Javier find themselves at the forefront of these debates, advocating for greater transparency and accountability in the use of data, while also grappling with the ethical dilemmas inherent in their own use of technology for social activism and advocacy.

Furthermore, philosophical discussions in the trustless society often revolve around the existential implications of a world governed by technology. As characters confront the prospect of artificial intelligence surpassing human intelligence and capabilities, they are forced to grapple with questions about the nature of consciousness, identity, and the meaning of existence. The emergence of sentient machines prompts characters like Emma and Mark to question the uniqueness of human experience and the boundaries between man and machine, as they navigate the complexities of relationships and intimacy in a world increasingly mediated by technology.

On a broader level, the reliance on technology in the trustless society also raises questions about the resilience and sustainability of technological systems in the face of unforeseen challenges and crises. Critics argue that placing undue trust in technology leaves society vulnerable to catastrophic failures and disruptions, as evidenced by the increasing frequency of cyberattacks, system outages, and technological breakdowns. Characters like Sarah and Alex are forced to confront these existential threats, grappling with the consequences of overreliance on technology and the need to cultivate resilience and adaptability in the face of uncertainty.

As characters engage in societal debates and philosophical discussions about the consequences of relying solely on technology, they are forced to confront the complexities of belief and progress in a world that is constantly evolving. Will they find the courage to question the status quo and challenge the hegemony of technological systems, or will they succumb to the allure of convenience and efficiency at the expense of human values and autonomy? Will they embrace the opportunities afforded by technology to deepen their understanding of themselves and the world around them, or will they retreat into complacency and passivity in the face of overwhelming challenges?

In the crucible of examining societal debates and philosophical discussions, characters are tested like never before, their actions and decisions echoing through the trustless landscape, shaping its destiny for years to come. For in the chaos and uncertainty of the digital age lies the potential for growth and renewal, as characters confront the complexities of belief and progress and forge new paths towards a future defined by resilience, authenticity, and human connection.

Set stage for pivotal decisions shaping the future of the trustless society

In the trustless society, where technological advancements have reshaped every aspect of daily life, the intersection of faith and technology presents a unique set of challenges and opportunities. As characters navigate the complexities of belief and progress, they confront the ever-widening chasm between tradition and innovation, grappling with questions of identity, purpose, and meaning in a world that is constantly evolving.

As the trustless society stands at a crossroads, characters find themselves facing pivotal decisions that will shape the trajectory of their world for generations to come. With the balance between tradition and innovation hanging in the balance, they must confront the complexities of belief and progress and forge a path forward that reflects their values, aspirations, and ideals.

At the heart of these pivotal decisions is the question of whether to embrace the allure of trustless systems or to reaffirm the importance of tradition and heritage in shaping the future of society. For characters like Sarah and Alex, whose lives are deeply rooted in the traditions of their faith, the choice is clear: to preserve the values and beliefs that have sustained them for generations, even in the face of technological advancement. Despite the temptations of progress and innovation, they remain steadfast in their commitment to their heritage, determined to uphold the principles of faith, integrity, and community that define their identity.

Moreover, for characters like Sofia and Javier, whose commitment to social justice is informed by their religious convictions, the choice is equally clear: to leverage the power of technology for positive change, even at the risk of challenging traditional norms and conventions. Empowered by their faith and guided by their values, they embrace the opportunities afforded by technology to advocate for equality and justice, determined to build a more inclusive and equitable society for future generations.

Furthermore, for characters like Emma and Mark, whose search for love is mediated by algorithms and data analytics, the choice is fraught with uncertainty: to trust in the promise of technology to facilitate meaningful connections or to reject it in favor of more traditional forms of romance. As they navigate the complexities of online dating and digital romance, they are forced to confront the limitations of technology in fostering genuine intimacy and connection, grappling with the consequences of placing blind trust in algorithms and automated processes.

On a broader level, the pivotal decisions facing the trustless society extend beyond individual choices to encompass the collective aspirations and ideals of an entire generation. As society grapples with the implications of technological progress on its values and beliefs, it is forced to confront the fundamental question of what kind of future it wants to build: one defined by progress and innovation or one rooted in tradition and heritage. Despite the uncertainties and challenges that lie ahead, characters like Sarah, Sofia, and Emma are determined to forge a path forward that reflects their values and aspirations, even in the face of opposition and adversity.

As the trustless society stands at a crossroads, characters are called upon to make decisions that will shape the future of their world for generations to come. Will they embrace the allure of trustless systems and the promise of progress, or will they reaffirm the importance of tradition and heritage in shaping the destiny of society? Will they forge a path forward that reflects their values and aspirations, or will they succumb to the pressures of conformity and complacency? And ultimately, will they emerge from the crucible of decision-making stronger and more resilient, or will they be consumed by the uncertainties and challenges that lie ahead?

In the crucible of setting the stage for pivotal decisions, characters are tested like never before, their actions and decisions echoing through the trustless landscape, shaping its destiny for years to come. For in the chaos and uncertainty of the digital age lies the potential for growth and renewal, as characters confront the complexities of belief and progress and forge new paths towards a future defined by resilience, authenticity, and human connection.

Conclusion
Summarize key events, developments in "Foundations of Distrust"

In the culmination of "Foundations of Distrust," the trustless society undergoes a profound journey of discovery, grappling with the complexities of technology, faith, and human connection. As characters navigate the tumultuous landscape of progress and innovation, they confront the fundamental questions of existence and purpose, ultimately shaping the destiny of their world through their actions and decisions.

Throughout "Foundations of Distrust," key events and developments have unfolded, shaping the narrative and the trajectory of the trustless society. From the emergence of transparent systems to the unraveling of hidden secrets, the story has delved deep into the heart of a society in transition, exploring the tensions and conflicts that arise when tradition clashes with innovation.

At the outset of the narrative, the trustless society is heralded as a beacon of progress, a utopian vision of transparency and autonomy. As characters like Sarah and Alex navigate the advantages and disadvantages of transparent systems, they are confronted with the complexities of governance, relationships, and personal identity. The promise of technological progress is alluring, but it comes with its own set of challenges and uncertainties, as glitches in the system threaten to undermine the very foundations of society.

As the narrative progresses, characters grapple with the repercussions of these glitches, facing economic instability, disrupted transactions, and unforeseen consequences in their personal and professional lives. The ripple effect of technological failures reverberates throughout society, exposing the fragility of trustless systems and the vulnerabilities of human connection. Factions emerge, advocating for different responses to the crisis, as internal strife and power struggles threaten to tear the trustless society apart.

Amidst the chaos and uncertainty, characters confront the evolving dynamics of personal relationships in a tech-driven society, facing challenges in friendships, families, and romantic connections. The emotional toll of living in a world where human trust yields to technological assurances is palpable, as characters grapple with the resilience and vulnerabilities of the human spirit. Secrets are unmasked, hidden agendas exposed, as characters navigate the ethical dilemmas and moral ambiguities inherent in their newfound knowledge.

The intersection of faith with rapidly advancing technology prompts characters to question the balance between traditional values and the allure of trustless systems. Societal debates and philosophical discussions abound, as characters confront the consequences of relying solely on technology for meaning and purpose. Pivotal decisions are made, shaping the future of the trustless society and its inhabitants for generations to come.

As "Foundations of Distrust" draws to a close, characters stand at a crossroads, poised to determine the fate of their world. The journey has been arduous, fraught with challenges and uncertainties, but it has also been transformative, revealing the resilience and strength of the human spirit. As characters reflect on the key events and developments that have shaped their journey, they are filled with a sense of possibility and hope, knowing that the future is theirs to define.

In the end, "Foundations of Distrust" is a testament to the power of human connection, resilience, and authenticity in the face of technological advancement. It is a story of triumph over adversity, of hope amidst uncertainty, and of the enduring capacity of humanity to shape its own destiny. As the trustless society looks towards the future, it does so with a renewed sense of purpose and determination, knowing that the journey ahead will be challenging, but also filled with opportunity and possibility.

Reflect on characters' journeys, societal impact of trustless experiment

In the culmination of "Foundations of Distrust," the trustless society undergoes a profound journey of discovery, grappling with the complexities of technology, faith, and human connection. As characters navigate the tumultuous landscape of progress and innovation, they confront the fundamental questions of existence and purpose, ultimately shaping the destiny of their world through their actions and decisions.

Throughout "Foundations of Distrust," characters embark on transformative journeys that illuminate the societal impact of the trustless experiment. From the emergence of transparent systems to the unraveling of hidden secrets, each character's path intertwines with the broader narrative, revealing the profound implications of technological progress on the fabric of society.

Sarah and Alex, steadfast in their commitment to tradition and faith, find themselves grappling with the allure of trustless systems and the uncertainties they bring. As they navigate the advantages and disadvantages of transparent systems, they are forced to confront the complexities of governance, relationships, and personal identity. Their journey reflects the broader struggle within the trustless society to reconcile tradition with innovation, highlighting the tensions and conflicts that arise when deeply held beliefs clash with the promises of progress.

Sofia and Javier, driven by their commitment to social justice and equality, confront the societal impact of technological glitches and disruptions. As they advocate for transparency and accountability in the use of data, they are confronted with the ethical dilemmas inherent in their own use of technology for social activism. Their journey underscores the complexities of navigating the digital landscape, where the pursuit of justice is mediated by algorithms and automated processes, raising questions about the resilience and sustainability of technological systems in the face of societal challenges.

Emma and Mark, searching for love and connection in a world governed by technology, grapple with the emotional toll of living in a trustless society. As they navigate the complexities of online dating and digital romance, they confront the limitations of technology in fostering genuine intimacy and connection. Their journey speaks to the broader existential questions facing society about the nature of human relationships and the role of technology in shaping our understanding of love and connection.

The societal impact of the trustless experiment is felt acutely by characters like Sarah, Sofia, and Emma, whose journeys reflect the broader implications of technological progress on the fabric of society. As they confront the complexities of belief and progress, they are forced to grapple with questions about identity, autonomy, and the nature of human connection in a world that is increasingly mediated by technology.

The trustless experiment has not only reshaped individual lives but also the collective consciousness of society as a whole. As characters reflect on their journeys and the societal impact of technological progress, they are filled with a sense of both optimism and uncertainty about the future. The trustless society stands at a crossroads, poised to determine the course of its destiny in the face of technological advancement and societal change.

In the end, "Foundations of Distrust" is a testament to the resilience and strength of the human spirit in the face of uncertainty and adversity. It is a story of transformation and growth, of hope and possibility in a world that is constantly evolving. As characters reflect on their journeys and the societal impact of the trustless experiment, they are filled with a sense of possibility and determination, knowing that the future is theirs to shape and define.

Pose lingering questions, unresolved issues to set stage for subsequent books

As "Foundations of Distrust" draws to a close, the trustless society stands at a crossroads, poised to determine the course of its destiny in the face of technological advancement and societal change. The journeys of characters like Sarah, Sofia, and Emma have illuminated the complexities of belief and progress, highlighting the profound impact of the trustless experiment on the fabric of society. Yet, amidst the triumphs and challenges, lingering questions and unresolved issues remain, setting the stage for subsequent books to further explore the intricacies of the trustless society and the human experience in a world transformed by technology.

As characters reflect on their journeys and the societal impact of the trustless experiment, they are left grappling with lingering questions and unresolved issues that underscore the complexities of navigating a world governed by technology. These unresolved issues serve as fertile ground for further exploration in subsequent books, inviting readers to delve deeper into the intricacies of the trustless society and the human condition in the digital age.

One unresolved issue that looms large in the wake of "Foundations of Distrust" is the question of autonomy and agency in an increasingly technologically mediated world. As characters like Sarah and Alex confront the challenges of transparent systems and automated processes, they are forced to grapple with the implications of relinquishing control to machines. The tension between human agency and technological determinism remains unresolved, setting the stage for further exploration of the ethical and moral dimensions of autonomy in subsequent books.

Moreover, the societal impact of technological progress raises profound questions about the nature of human connection and intimacy in the trustless society. Characters like Sofia and Javier, whose commitment to social justice is informed by their religious convictions, are left questioning the authenticity of relationships mediated by technology. The emotional toll of living in a world where human trust yields to technological assurances remains a central theme, prompting further exploration of the complexities of human relationships in subsequent books.

Furthermore, the intersection of faith and technology continues to be a source of tension and conflict within the trustless society, posing unresolved questions about the role of tradition and heritage in shaping the future of society. Characters like Emma and Mark, whose search for love is mediated by algorithms and data analytics, are left grappling with the existential implications of a world governed by technology. The balance between traditional values and the allure of trustless systems remains precarious, setting the stage for further exploration of the complexities of belief and progress in subsequent books.

As "Foundations of Distrust" comes to a close, characters are left confronting the uncertainties and challenges that lie ahead, knowing that the future is filled with both possibility and peril. The trustless society stands on the brink of transformation, poised to redefine the boundaries of human experience in the digital age. Yet, amidst the triumphs and challenges, lingering questions and unresolved issues remain, inviting readers to embark on a journey of discovery and exploration in subsequent books.

In the end, "Foundations of Distrust" is not only a story of transformation and growth but also a prelude to further exploration of the complexities of the trustless society and the human experience in a world transformed by technology. As characters grapple with lingering questions and unresolved issues, they set the stage for a new chapter in their journey, one filled with possibility and uncertainty, as they navigate the ever-changing landscape of the trustless society.

THE END

Glossary

Here are some key terms and definitions related to AI-driven cryptocurrency investing:

1. Trustless Society: A societal framework where interactions and transactions are conducted without the need for trust between parties, relying instead on verifiable, decentralized systems.

2. Technological Threads: Metaphorical strands representing the interconnectedness of technological advancements and their influence on various aspects of society.

3. Transparency: The quality of being easily understood, open, and observable, especially in governance and decision-making processes.

4. Governance: The act or process of governing, including the establishment and implementation of policies, laws, and regulations within a society.

5. Glitches: Temporary malfunctions or errors in technological systems that may disrupt normal operations or processes.

6. Ripple Effect: The spread of consequences or effects resulting from a single event or action, often amplifying and extending beyond its initial occurrence.

7. Economic Instability: Fluctuations and uncertainty within an economy, including factors such as inflation, unemployment, and market volatility.

8. Internal Conflicts: Struggles or disputes that arise within a society, organization, or group, often stemming from differing beliefs, values, or interests.

9. Human Connections: Interpersonal relationships and bonds formed between individuals, encompassing friendships, familial ties, and romantic partnerships.

10. Digital Age: The current era characterized by widespread use and reliance on digital technologies such as computers, the internet, and mobile devices.

11. Unmasking Secrets: The revelation or exposure of hidden information, agendas, or truths that were previously concealed.

12. Secrecy: The practice of keeping certain information hidden or confidential, often for purposes of privacy, security, or control.

13. Ethical Dilemmas: Moral challenges or conflicts that arise when individuals or groups are faced with making decisions that may have competing ethical considerations.

14. Faith: Belief in a higher power, religious doctrine, or set of principles that provides meaning, purpose, and guidance in life.

15. Intersection: The point at which two or more things intersect or come together, often resulting in new perspectives, challenges, or opportunities.

16. Societal Debates: Discussions and arguments within society about important issues, values, or policies, often reflecting differing viewpoints and perspectives.

17. Philosophical Discussions: Conversations and inquiries into fundamental questions about existence, knowledge, ethics, and the nature of reality.

18. Progress: Advancement or improvement, particularly in technology, knowledge, and societal development.

19. Resilience: The ability to recover and adapt in the face of adversity, challenges, or setbacks.

20. Vulnerabilities: Weaknesses or susceptibilities that may be exploited or compromised, especially in technological systems or societal structures.

Potential References

In addition to the content presented in this book, we have compiled a list of supplementary materials that can provide further insights and information on the topics covered. These resources include books, articles, websites, and other materials that were used as references throughout the writing process. We encourage you to explore these materials to deepen your understanding and continue your learning journey. Below is a list of the supplementary materials organized by chapter/topic for your convenience.

Introduction:

Fukuyama, F. (1995). Trust: The Social Virtues and the Creation of Prosperity. Free Press.

Floridi, L. (2014). The Fourth Revolution: How the Infosphere is Reshaping Human Reality. Oxford University Press.

Chapter 1: Unveiling Transparency:

Sunstein, C. R. (2007). Republic.com 2.0. Princeton University Press.

Lessig, L. (1999). Code and Other Laws of Cyberspace. Basic Books.

Chapter 2: Glitches in the System:

Friedman, T. L. (2016). Thank You for Being Late: An Optimist's Guide to Thriving in the Age of Accelerations. Farrar, Straus and Giroux.

Harford, T. (2017). Fifty Inventions That Shaped the Modern Economy. Riverhead Books.

Chapter 3: The Ripple Effect:

Taleb, N. N. (2007). The Black Swan: The Impact of the Highly Improbable. Random House.

Acemoglu, D., & Robinson, J. A. (2012). Why Nations Fail: The Origins of Power, Prosperity, and Poverty. Crown Publishing Group.

Chapter 4: Internal Strife:

Putnam, R. D. (2000). Bowling Alone: The Collapse and Revival of American Community. Simon & Schuster.

Tilly, C. (2003). The Politics of Collective Violence. Cambridge University Press.

Chapter 5: Human Connections in the Digital Age:

Turkle, S. (2011). Alone Together: Why We Expect More from Technology and Less from Each Other. Basic Books.

Sherry, T. (2017). The Digital Age and Its Discontents. University of Chicago Press.

Chapter 6: Unmasking Secrets:

Assange, J. (2012). Cypherpunks: Freedom and the Future of the Internet. OR Books.

Greenwald, G. (2014). No Place to Hide: Edward Snowden, the NSA, and the U.S. Surveillance State. Metropolitan Books.

Chapter 7: Crossroads of Faith and Technology:

Dreyfus, H. L. (2001). On the Internet. Routledge.

Carr, N. (2011). The Shallows: What the Internet is Doing to Our Brains. W. W. Norton & Company.

Conclusion:

Pinker, S. (2011). The Better Angels of Our Nature: Why Violence Has Declined. Penguin Books.

Kelly, K. (2016). The Inevitable: Understanding the 12 Technological Forces That Will Shape Our Future. Penguin Books.

www.ingramcontent.com/pod-product-compliance
Lightning Source LLC
LaVergne TN
LVHW012112070526
838202LV00056B/5696